MAHMOOD DORANAI

The Muslim's Handbook

Copyright © 2021 by Mahmood Doranai

All rights reserved. No part of this publication may be reproduced, stored or transmitted in any form or by any means, electronic, mechanical, photocopying, recording, scanning, or otherwise without written permission from the publisher. It is illegal to copy this book, post it to a website, or distribute it by any other means without permission.

Mahmood Doranai asserts the moral right to be identified as the author of this work.

First edition

This book was professionally typeset on Reedsy.
Find out more at reedsy.com

Contents

Preface   v
   The relevance and purpose of the book   vi
   The structure of the book   vii

I   PART ONE: IT STARTS WITH THINKING

1   Introduction   3
2   Thinking Big   10
   Why think big   10
   How to think big   11
     0. Ask 'valuable questions'.   11
     1. Think long-term, rather then short-term.   13
     2. Generalizing the purpose of the effort and struggle to other parts of life.   13
     3. Think in terms of processes, rather then outcomes.   14
     4. Treat failures with gratefulness, and employ it, to increase your ambitions.   14
     5. Asses / Evaluate / Judge / Treat things based on what they could be (i.e. based on their potential), not on what they are (present reality).   14
3   The Improvement Cycle   15
   Process View and System Thinking   18
     1. All work occurs in a system of interconnected processes.   18
     2. Variation exists in all processes.   19

3. Understanding and reducing complexity are keys to success.	20
The Improvement Cycle and Tools:	20
Further Reading	22
4 A Word On Power, And Its Projection	23
What is power?	23
What increases or diminishes it?	24
Components of Power	25
Knowledge	25
Communication	26
Alliances	26
Automation through institutions	26
Projection of Power	27
The Choice of Action	28
The Choice of Timing	28
The Choice of Tools and Techniques	29

II PART TWO: DESIGNING FOR SUPREMACY, NOT SURVIVAL

5 The Identity, Values And Symbolism Of The Ummah	33
The Traits of a Muslim and the Practices That Define Us	34
The Objection of the Kuffar	39
What We Muslims Can Do, to Better Assert Our Identity, Values and Practices	42
6 Education	48
The Requirements That Our Educational Systems, Institutions, Practices, Materials and Policies Should Meet	49
How a Novice Becomes an Expert	51
What We Can Do	51
Education of Technical Fields	51
Children's Education	53
Learning Platforms, Institutions and Practices	54

Dealing With Counter Forces and Scoring a Long Term Victory:	57
Further Reading	59
7 On Dawah and Islamic Activism	61
What We Can Do	63
The Basics	63
Dealing with Religious Innovations and Innovators	68
The Elite of Dawah	70
8 Human Resources, And Building Institutions	73
On Chaos, Order and Change	74
Common Causes of Organizational failures are:	75
Establishing Organizations	76
The organizational checklist:	77
HR Strategy of the Ummah and Managing Sensitive Projects	78
Exponentially increasing our power, and in a short time frame by connecting the different organizations, networks and communities.	79
9 Infrastructure And Environmental Design	81
The Purpose of Environmental and Infrastructural Upgrades	82
What We Can Do	83
Health Care	83
The Basics	83
Leisure and Recreational Infrastructure	84
Mental Health	85
Food Production and Storage	86
Replacing the Synthetic with the Natural	86
Hydroponics and Aeroponics	89
The Sahara Project	90
Similar projects can be undertaken in other parts of the world:	91
What Will This Achieve	92
On Sensitive Projects	93
10 Conclusion	95

From Defense To Offense   97
Epilogue   101

Preface

In the Name of Allah, the Merciful, the Compassionate
All praises belong to Allah, Lord of all the Worlds

This book is a product of ten years of thinking, writing, questioning, discovering, forgetting, rediscovering and rewriting. I have over the course of the past ten years (2012 - 2022), explored the causes, effects, processes, systems, institutions, biographies, human behavioral patterns, and historical cycles relevant to the present circumstances of the Muslim Ummah, and have attempted to find creative solutions and ways of communicating those solutions to the Ummah, in the hope that Allah may enlighten us to the means of coping with- and prospering through these difficulties.

There have been a great deal of scholarly writings, speeches, courses, seminars, and conferences exploring various ways of responding to our current challenges and the challenges faced by humanity at large. These works have explored in-depth the various aspects of the challenges, opportunities and choices that the Ummah is faced with. However, despite the great quality and quantity of such works, the Islamic Civilization has continued to be inundated with problems — both of the old variety, and by many new kinds. In this book I have attempted to summarize the ten years of research, and have chosen to present it in a simple and concise way, seeking by it the Forgiveness and Pleasure of Allah, The All Hearing, The All Seeing.

The relevance and purpose of the book

The book presents more then [***the number of ideas, that you should count***] of practical ideas and steps that individual Muslims and Islamic organizations and institutions of many categories can take to:

1. Break the psychological barriers of the Ummah, and reveal the inevitability of global Islamic supremacy
2. Facilitate conversation
3. Control and minimize uncertainty by Allah's Permission
4. Assert Islamic sovereignty, values, and establish Islamic practices and symbols — and through them provide means of coping with chaos
5. Facilitate independent and inter-dependent decision-making across Muslim communities, organizations, and institutions.
6. Make Muslims completely independent of the Kuffar, and take complete control of the Muslims' affairs, eliminating any room for the intrusions of the Kuffar

Both the experienced, and occasional reader will In Shaa Allah find, that the uniqueness and value of the book lies in its rare combinations of simplicity of language, the great number and variety of ideas, the high practical utility of those ideas and guidance, the shortness of the book, and its unique style, given that the book does not focus on the things that *should* be done, but rather on *all the things that **could** be done* to improve the situation of the Ummah.

I ask Allah to purify our intentions and accepts our good deeds, and reward us greatly in this life and the Hereafter.

The structure of the book

In Part I, I have attempted to raise the awareness of the reader to some important thinking processes and patterns that we can use to our benefit. The *Introduction* presents the big picture view of the content of the book, and is going to prime the readers mind for the ideas presented throughout the book, thus making the reading a proactive experience.

Part II comprises the meat of this book. Each chapter presents creative practical solutions to the issues that the Ummah, and humanity at large are facing in that particular area. Since all of the chapters are self-contained, the impatient reader may jump directly to the chapter in the second part of the book, for immediate insight and benefit. Each chapter starts with introductory remarks, and ends with the set of ideas and solutions, provided in a bullet point format.

All ideas, questions, solutions and discussions in this book, are to be viewed in the context of each other. Only then will the reader be able to identify and take the most valuable gems provided in this book.

In the epilogue, I list a few things that I have chosen to leave out of this book for various reasons. I also encourage the reader to look forward to my future works, in which those topics will be addressed.

I

PART ONE: IT STARTS WITH THINKING

Success in crisis situations requires productive thinking patterns.

What are the things that we have been missing in our practice of problem identification, structuring, classification, description, prediction and solution generation?

In the first part of the book, I present - among other things, the practice and art of thinking big, an understanding of how improvement cycles work, and a practical understanding of power.

1

Introduction

In The Name of Allah, The Most Merciful, The Most Gracious

The attempts of Muslims so far at rebuilding the Islamic World, and reestablishing it as the supreme power that it once was, have been highly unorganized – hence, inefficient. This has caused the Ummah countless humiliations, and suffering at the hands of the Kuffar and misguided Muslims. In this work, I hope to provide a part of the remedy, required for elevating the morale of the Ummah and addressing the many sources of chaos and uncertainty, that have been encroaching on Muslims from all directions.

Many writings, conferences, and lectures have attempted to list the various things that *should* be done to reclaim our position as leaders of the world. Some, if not many, of these attempts have been successful (Alhamdulillah), and have as a result led to the rapid rise in the number of converts to Islam – and at the same time, the sophistication of the Muslim mind. However, Muslims – despite our great numbers and improved educational level, seem to have grown less confident in our ways of life, and more accepting and tolerant of the arrogant ways of the West and their 'values'.

For the sake of greater productivity, we Muslims have to deal not just with the question of, *what should be done* – but also, *what are all the possible things that* **could** *be done,* to raise the Ummah to the top of the civilizational dominance hierarchy. The difference between the 'should' and the 'could' approaches is, that the latter is more holistic and conducive for creative problem structuring, brainstorming and problem solving. It addresses the more general question of, *what do we* **want**, rather then the more specific *problem* of *what do we* **need**. If we are to arrive at the desired goals, we have to grab **any** opportunity for improvement that we can possibly grab, rather then wait and/or endlessly keep planning for those few opportunities that we would have to grab at some point or another to meet our needs as a civilization.

It is my understanding and conviction, that there is a need for a more aggressive, holistic, decentralized and hands-on approach to improvement, as opposed to the anxiety ridden and appeasement oriented approach that we have mostly relied on, since the fall of the Usmani Khilafa. Asking the right question (what *could* be done?), is the first, and most important step towards a brighter future In Shaa Allah.

In addition to a comprehensive list of opportunities that we must create – we also need operational guidance and guidelines for the successful initiation, monitoring and evaluation of the improvement process. For people to learn, act and operate efficiently, they must not only be given advice on *what* they should do, but also *when, how* and *in what order* they should execute the required procedures to get closer to the desired outcomes. In order for a rapid change to take place, we Muslims must ponder over *all* the possibilities and opportunities for improvement - regardless of the significance of the individual ideas. Indeed the solution to our crisis might lie in a large number of 'insignificant' ideas, then in a small number of 'great' ideas. Many small steps, when taken in combination towards an end goal tend to have a synergistic effect on one another. To aid us in this mission, I have attempted to provide a starting point, a framework of a sort, for effective thinking, and a guide for immediate action on the many fronts, where we need to be advancing.

INTRODUCTION

The approach taken in the book is a practical, pragmatic and prescription oriented. It is my understanding and assumption, that the nature and scale of the challenges is clear to most Muslims - hence I have avoided the redundant descriptions (wherever possible) of the problems that we face and the multitude of their causes. Hence, the book doesn't address the spiritual and religious shortcomings of Muslims – which have been extensively and eloquently addressed by the u'lama and Muslim academics across the globe. The main goal – though not the only one, which I attempt to reach with these few pages is, to provide a set of **practical steps** that Muslims, and Islamic organizations can take, in order to capitalize on the available opportunities, and initiate various positive feedback-loops that would ensure a self-sustaining process of improvement.

For any improvement process to succeed, it must be preceded by the accumulation of intelligent and insightful questions. Such questions should be free from uninformed and/or misinformed assumptions; they should arouse our curiosity, ambition, and creativity of Muslims. Such questions, are themselves inspiring, provide motivation, encouragement, and structure to what would be otherwise an unmanageable (if not unfruitful) struggle towards our desired goals. By simply asking the right questions, in the right context – we can gain great insight into the nature of the seemingly incomprehensible.

To prime the reader's mind, I have provided some questions below, which I hope the reader would contemplate over, before moving on to the presented ideas and solutions.

In no particular order, these questions are:

Because of the propaganda against Islam and the demoralization of Muslims – we have internalized repression and demoralization. How do we censor, stop and eliminate such attempts at the programming of the Muslim mind? What are the various tools, techniques and strategies which non-Muslims have adopted for this mission?

How do we become proactive thinkers and actors - rather then continue being passive observers and impulsive reactionaries?

How do we increase the productivity of Muslim communities and organizations - and step by step, reacquire our strength and confidence?

What are the relationships between our personal decisions, and the well being of the Ummah.

The Muslim Ummah is weak at the moment, what are the repercussions – if Muslims continue to be weak?

Assuming that over the long run, chaos is unavoidable – how should we prepare for/against it? What necessary procedures, organizational and cultural structures we must put in place, in-order to address the chaos quickly and efficiently? What are the skills, qualities and areas of knowledge that we must foster in ourselves and especially in our youth, in order to make The Word of Allah Supreme.

We know that Islam will overtake every way of life — sooner, rather then later; but what are the attitudes that we must get rid of in our personal lives, community and cultural norms, before this change can be realized?

How, and when should we address the decisions of our governments that go completely against the overall interest of the society, and especially those rulings / laws that go completely against Islam and Muslims; such as the invasions of Muslim lands; the financing, recruitment, intelligence assistance and protection of the radical groups; the unequal taxing policies for the rich, and the middle class; the nepotism in the justice system etc.?

In our attempts to improve our situation, what are the sacrifices that we need to make, that we are to weary of making? Where does this resistance to the prophetic guidance stem from? How do we address it? And who / where are

INTRODUCTION

the (cognitively) resourceful people who can rise up to address it?

Education and knowledge are *the* fundamental prerequisites for prosperity (both material and spiritual) and for surpassing our current limitations; And since we are and have been losing grip on our reality, it no doubt implies, that something is wrong with our educational systems. What are these deficiencies? And what kind of organizational and pedagogical reforms are needed to realign ourselves with the prophetic wisdom, with which Allah turned the illiterate and impoverished Arabs into the masters of civilizations?

Our resources – both tangible and intangible (time, money, talent, natural resources etc..) are limited: what are the things that we should prioritize? And why? In other words, what are the small, easy and inexpensive projects and changes that we can first focus on (implement, undertake) that would bring about the greatest positive change? What are those projects / changes that would start the positive feed-back loops in our societies?

Stories are one of the best tools for shaping human thought and behavior; what are the stories that we have been telling ourselves, and the stories that those around us (including our adversaries) have been imposing on us - that have been doing us harm? And what are the stories that we need to tell, and indeed, write that would help us deal with the chaos much more productively? What are the stories that will help us see the world in a newer way? A way that would let us see the world and the various trends (political, cultural, economical, scientific and technological) for what they really are – not just what / how they are portrayed to be—either by its detractors or its proponents? What are these trends? Who started them, and how have they affected different segments of the global population, and most especially the youth of the world?

Self-blaming for the chaos can be both productive and destructive; Where do we draw the line between our own doing and the doing of others as far as their sinister schemes, tactics and intentions are concerned with respect to –

first of all the Ummah, and then, the global middle and lower classes? How do we undo the agency of the non-Muslim elite on our mind, well being and religio-political affairs?

What processes and practices will increase our self-agency and self-efficacy? What changes in our attitudes, policies and HR management can repel the psychological, economic, military, intelligence and political attacks on the Muslim Ummah?

Environment plays a critical role in our mood, behavior and long-term well being; Because of the prevalence of mental health problems in the Muslim World, and Muslim communities across the globe – it is clear that some of the chaos can be attributed to the poor environment; What are the environmental variables that we have to manipulate in order to address/minimize the material and spiritual poverty of the Muslim World?

Corruption in all of its forms - be it nepotism, bribing, sexual harassment, rapes, spousal and child abuse, substance abuse, human trafficking, are a daily reality across the world, and in some cases, most rampant in the Muslim World; How do the overall societal processes, systems, and organizations get affected by the different forms of corruption - both short term and long term? Are there any variables, which when altered slightly, could lead to rapid decline in crime - and the circumstances that partly give rise to them?

What are the various assumptions that Muslim minorities have in non-Muslim majority countries about their own role, and responsibilities to the Ummah, and the world more generally? How is the situation of the Muslim reverts in these societies, and their role in the local Muslim community? How do all of these assumptions affect their short-term productivity, and long-term well being and safety (physical, financial and spiritual)?

How can we capitalize on the newer technologies that will be shaping the future of humanity, such as nanotechnology, MEMS technology, quantum

INTRODUCTION

computing, novel manufacturing techniques, and engineering processes, such as laser additive printing; Atomic, and optical science techniques, such as laser enrichment of isotopes, high efficiency solar panels, artificial intelligence, biotechnology, and computational sciences?

These are *some* of the relevant questions that we have to keep on the table, while strategizing for a better tomorrow. The reader should come up with their own set of questions, and share and discuss them with others in order to get a more comprehensive map of the problems, and the possible opportunities and solutions.

Answering all, or many of these questions is beyond the scope of this book, but I have still included the questions here, in order to prime the readers' mind for some of the answers, and ideas provided in the book - and many others that I will be addressing in my future works In Shaa Allah. The least I hope this book can do for the reader, is to provide a practicing ground for constructive, solution oriented way of thinking. These questions, and the ideas provided in the rest of the book should help spark the readers' creative ambitions, and the desire to explore further on their own.

To begin with, we have to think big…

2

Thinking Big

Why think big

In order for us, to recover from the nightmares of recent past - we have to first imagine, visualize, and simulate in our minds, the possible realities that we can create with the help of Allah. We have to first imagine all those actions that we need to take, to establish control over our reality, *before* we can actually act, and implement the various improvement programs. The greater the *value* of the simulated/visualized realities - the more likely we are to **act** in a way, that would bring as closer to the desired reality. Initially the goal oriented behavior is conscious, and requires some thinking and calculation. But the sharper images of the desired goals become in our minds, and the more we relate them to our past and present - the more automatized the goal oriented behavior becomes.

To determine the value of the possible realities - we need to first analyze our psychological makeup. We have to recognize, that the human psychological makeup and the behavioral patterns that it gives rise to - are highly sensitive to *novelty*. That is, we evaluate all available options according to various criteria, to determine their value. And the criteria that tends to influence our decision making process/behavior the most, is novelty. The more novel the goal, the more likely we are to pursue it. The sharper the images of the goal and the visuals of us taking the required steps towards it, the more likely we are to succeed in achieving that goal In Shaa Allah. And so - before we start acting, we have to carefully choose, and visualize those changes, that we wish to realize.

In this chapter I provide guidance, on how to set high goals, and generate valuable ideas.

How to think big

While most people seem to understand *why* we need to think big, only a few seem to have a clear conception of *how to think big*. Given that *thinking big* is the first requirement for *acting big (i.e. making big things happen)*, we have to first make the imagination and visualization of our goals, and the steps that lead to those goals, a routine. For optimal learning I see it necessary to describe the process of how to think big.

The following points describe the process of thinking big:

0. Ask 'valuable questions'.

The single most important step in generating *high value* ideas, is the zeroth step – *asking* the right questions. If one undermines the value of this step, and does not give it it's due attention, you can be certain that the end result of the brainstorming would be unimpressive. Before everything else, we must brainstorm valuable questions – questions that in and of-themselves are unique and insightful. The following are some characteristics of such questions:

- They spark your imagination, and divert your attention to the countless possibilities and opportunities. They highlight the things that you can control, and thus make the burden of not knowing something, much more bearable. They undo those assumptions that an individual, community or organization might have about their present and past realities, and experiences. And they highlight the many ways the concerned entities can alter present realities, and create new ones.

- Valuable questions are those, which by simply asking them, will increase our motivation, by helping to organize our thoughts into a coherent and consistent structure, thus giving us an order of operation or action — starting with the simplest and easiest step that can be taken, to the most involved and difficult ones.

- They increase our productivity, by eliminating counter-productive thought processes and anxiety. This occurs when the same problems are grouped in multiple ways, into multiple different classes and categories (e.g. simple vs. complicated; concrete vs. abstract; immediate vs. non-essential).

- They are more holistic; that is - they establish, and highlight the relationship of the given problem with other problems, thus exposing any assumptions, misconception, and ideas, that we might not have been aware of. Good questions take into account the evolution (or history) of the problems, and the known solutions. Undoubtedly any problem that we might be facing, has been faced before by countless other people, across time, and across geographies; If not the same problem, then surely *similar* problems have been experienced by others during past ages. Good questions connect the known realities of the past, with human generated alternative realities i.e. fiction; Which fictional works deal with similar issues as those, relevant to the problem solvers' context? Putting ideas, problems, questions, processes in a greater context - allows us to see the historical cycles, and patterns relevant to our current problems.

1. Think long-term, rather then short-term.

Don't let your short-term solutions, to your minor problems, be the cause of major problems to the next actor, organization or generation of people.

2. Generalizing the purpose of the effort and struggle to other parts of life.

By generalizing the purpose of your effort to multiple domains of life, you are exponentially increasing the value of the goal, and are thus more likely to pursue it. Example: I am learning programming, not just so I can find a job and earn a living – but also, to teach others; to automate countless repetitive tasks in my personal life; to maintain and increase my own cognitive capacity; to have fun; to contribute to the democratization of knowledge, through open source projects etc.

3. Think in terms of processes, rather then outcomes.

Enjoy the ideas, procedures and challenges, that you are engaged with and don't over-contemplate the results that are expected of you. You need to know approximately where you are headed, but while working towards that goal on daily basis, you are better off thinking about the next one hour, rather then the next one month or year.

4. Treat failures with gratefulness, and employ it, to increase your ambitions.

If you failed in acquiring something, take a short break, and reevaluate your options. Add a few extra things to your wish list. By increasing the value of your purpose/goal, you are recharging your motivation, and increasing your creativity, thus revealing possibilities that you weren't aware of previously.

5. Asses / Evaluate / Judge / Treat things based on what they could be (i.e. based on their potential), not on what they are (present reality).

These are some important considerations when planning a change. Others, we will explore as we progress through the chapters.

Big ideas by themselves, don't guarantee improvement. They must be put to use in the right way, at the right time, in the right combinations, and at times, by the right people. This is the topic of the next two chapters.

3

The Improvement Cycle

> **Go forth, whether light or heavy, and strive with your wealth and your lives in the cause of Allah. That is better for you, if you only knew.** Quran 9:41

The previous chapter explored the *why*, and *how* of thinking big. In-order for us to trigger and manage rapid changes, we need to make *vivid* in our minds those processes that would bring us closer to our destiny.

> **It is He who has sent His Messenger with guidance and the religion of truth to manifest it over all religion, although they who associate others with Allah dislike it.** Quran 9:33

In this chapter we will grapple with the questions of *when* and *where* (i.e. the context) of thinking big. To start with, we have to realize that our problems as a civilization, are nothing unique. Everything that we are seeing, and experiencing has been witnessed in the past by other societies, nations, civilizations, businesses, educational organizations, and social movements. This implies at least two things:

1. We can always find our solutions in the books of history.
2. Any attempts at improving our circumstances, must always be preceded by a study of relevant historical literature of similar phenomenon, before we start laying our plans for actions.

To appreciate the significance of a context for problem solving and learning (i.e. *when* and *where* of thinking big), we can take a look at an example from recent history; What happens, when sound thinking is absent from the problem solving processes? What happens, when people are confronted with complex processes and systems - the complexity of which, they fail to appreciate? And what happens, when we only ask *what to do* and *how to do it* - without having also explored, *what NOT to do* and *WHEN, WHERE and WHY not to do it!*

Here is a good example of what failing to understand the context of a problem looks like: The USA's War On Drugs eliminated drugs labs from its soil, and led to the killing and imprisonment of a high number of criminals. And that, according to the policy makers' understanding should have put an end to America's drug problems. But it didn't. The War On Drugs merely drove drugs production from the US, into Mexico. The strategy that was supposed to deliver a death blow to drugs related crimes and consumption - turned out to be a most *viscous* catalyst for the *exact opposite* of what was expected; Drugs smuggling and consumption, and its devastating effects only increased, leading to the ravaging of many American communities. The War On Drugs shifted the production of drugs to lower income regions, where it could be produced for cheaper, and in larger quantities, thus triggering a major rise in its consumption in the neighboring US.

How could this have possibly happened? Not paying attention to the context, nature or the *when* and *where* of the problem, is a sure way to destroy *that very thing*, that one was striving to protect, and to *undo* that very progress, that was considered insufficient. The American decision makers failed to distinguish between local, regional and global problems. Not knowing the scope of a problem - but still implementing strategies to solve it, is a *guaranteed way* to make problems *worse*, rather then solving them. Not knowing where, and when to start - and where and when to stop, *but* still wanting to act is a most efficient strategy for self-destruction. In the case of the US, they were attempting to solve a *global* problem with *local* strategies. Drugs trafficking and production is a *global* problem. It might have local consequences, but it's solution strategy cannot *just* be local. Without a process view, it is often difficult to define the scope, and primary sources of the problem.

It is this lack of process view, that has been the cause of turf wars among Muslims ('the problem is with them, not us'), leading to great deal of frustration, because of the lack of coordination of efforts, the hurdles in the way of sharing of useful, relevant information - and the failure of protecting, connecting, networking, and strengthening the various groups of Muslim scholars, influencers, du'at, artists, scientists, military thinkers, businessmen and politicians.

In this chapter I have provided some necessary guidance, that will help us In Shaa Allah avoid these common, and destructive pitfalls in our thinking. The main message that I wish to get across, is that everything we think, say or do - has to be guided by all the relevant information we can possibly access. The remaining sections of this chapter can be summarized in the following three points:

1. Process simplification is often a major contributor to improvement.
2. Productive change management requires the modeling, quantification and systematic reduction of complexity and variation.

3. The new improvement ideas, solution and strategies have to be piloted on a smaller scale, before they can be implemented a larger wider scale.

Process View and System Thinking

Process and/or system thinking is an approach to learning and a tool for guiding actions, and it is based on the following principles:

1. All work occurs in a system of interconnected processes.

In order to increase our productivity, we must consider the system as a whole, rather then sub-optimizing its individual components, without the necessary process related data to guide and aid our decisions.

We Muslims have failed consistently when we have tried to increase our efficiency and power by addressing each problem independently, without the necessary context that is often provided by other problems.

Ignoring the inter-dependencies, and rich interactions between the various sub-processes and components of a larger, more complex system has landed us in greater chaos and inefficiencies.

For success, each sub-process must be investigated in the context of other processes to identify areas of opportunities, and improvement that will benefit the entire Ummah.

The first step is to identify the process or processes involved in our struggle.

Nothing will improve until we start documenting our processes and the critical process steps from which they are composed.

2. Variation exists in all processes.

Variation enters when operational procedures are not standardized or the role of the individual or units/groups is not aligned with the overall objective of the Ummah.

Variation and/or complexity is everywhere. Helping Muslims understand this fundamental principle, is a requisite step towards higher self-efficacy - both on an individual level, and on an organizational level. This is a contribution, that only the statistically literate can make to the Ummah. Every Muslim engaged in academic, consultancy and leadership activity has to master statistical thinking, and statistical methods, because problem description, and solution prescription, both depend on a good understanding of patterns and exceptions to those patterns - the subject matter of statistics.

The typical sources of complexity and/or variation are:

- **People:** different attitudes, different ways of doing things, different interests, different skills and abilities and different ways of communicating.
- **Methods:** Poorly described, documented and defined procedures, their timing, scope, interactivity and continuity.
- **Tools and Materials:** The use of different tools, different materials (physical, literary, data etc.).

3. Understanding and reducing complexity are keys to success.

To this end, we must establish standard processes for acquiring, and analyzing information concerning the various processes / systems / organizations, and their performance; as well as keeping tracks of the variables that affect the efficiency of these processes, delivering it to the relevant decision makers to aid in appropriate actions.

Reducing variation / complexity of the system / processes requires that we not only ask 'Why?' – which is important for *understanding* the process, but not necessarily in *guiding actions,* we must also ask *'How?', 'Where?', 'Using what tools?',* and *'Under what conditions?'.*

A good mnemonic for these steps is **SIPOC; S**uppliers provide **I**nputs to **P**rocesses that produce **O**utputs or products that go to **C**lients. Stated simply, we must figure out the SIPOC's of the Ummah, in-order to aid us in formulating efficient actions plans.

The Improvement Cycle and Tools:

- **Describe the system, the relationships between its individual components, and the tasks which it performs.** Describe and asses the processes using flowcharts, histograms, mind maps, algorithms (pseudo-code) etc. Failure to model the processes, allows for the ignorance of the thinkers, and decision makers at all levels of the organization / system / society, to go unnoticed, unquestioned and unrectified, and thus puts hurdles in the way of controlling the system.

THE IMPROVEMENT CYCLE

- **Identify the necessary resources** (learning resources, physical materials, information systems/resources and human resources), standards, attitudes and cultural norms that you would need, in order to propel the system in the desired direction.

- **Collect Data on key process variables.**

- **Identify the different sources and manifestations of variation:** Describe the variation of the results with respect to time, methods, tools, context / circumstances and actors. Using information modeling tools and techniques (cause and effect diagrams, computational models, simulations, geographic information systems etc.). Identify the desired end goal, state or result. Calculate the level and type of variation that would be required to reach that state. The variation will have to be decreased in certain areas and increased in others.

- **Reduce variation where possible.**

- **Increase variation where useful and/or necessary.**

- **Establish standard operational procedures:** If standards do not exist, then by definition everything is acceptable. Thus, to model and reduce complexity, we have to ask the following important questions: Are there standard ways of acquiring, analyzing, recording, protecting and sharing information? Are there specialized tools, people and institutions for carrying out these tasks in a timely fashion? Are there standard protocols of communication and sharing between the people and the institutions? How much capability and flexibility do these protocols afford the system? In other words – how resilient vs. fragile is the system? How quickly and efficiently can it respond to major changes in the environment?

- **Repeat.**

Further Reading

Improving Performance Through *Statistical Thinking* — ASQ Statistics Division, Authors: Galen C. Britz, Donald W. Emerling, Lynne B. Hare, Roger W. Hoerl, Stuart J. Janis, Janice E. Shade

4

A Word On Power, And Its Projection

At the heart of the Muslims' failures has been a lack of understanding of a most central concept – *power*. For us to succeed in our efforts, we have to understand power, the components that make it up, and the various ways of projecting it.

What is power?

Power is the ability to cause a desirable change in one's environment with intention, at the desired time, to the desired extent, with the chosen resources, imprinting on the minds and behavior of other players (both friends and adversaries) the desired impressions - while at the same time, not starting or accentuating undesirable chain of events, processes, or increasing the power of entities adversarial to one's own cause.

What increases or diminishes it?

Depending on the circumstances, power is diminished or increased by:

- **Its concentration or distribution:** If the challenges faced by the entity (be it an individual or an organization) are large in number, and multitude in variety, then power is *increased* by its distribution across players (allies, and at occasions adversaries) and across time i.e. all resources are not put to use at once, rather there are always resources that are kept in reserve, only to be put to work when the game (the behaviors, intentions and plans of other, and the resulting environment) becomes more comprehensible. If however, the challenges faced by the entity are great in magnitude, but small in variety, then power is *diminished* by its distribution to others, and its distribution over time - and *increased* by its concentration in the hand of that branch of the organization, or those individuals who have the expertise in those specific domains, in which the challenges appear, and which they have to be addressed.

- **Victory or loss:** After the resolution of conflicts, if the victory ends up increasing the burden of the victor, and decreases his ability to maneuver in the different domains of competition - then, the victory will have *diminished* his power. But if the victory leads to greater resources and assets — both tangible and intangible, such that it would at the bare minimum provide some guidance, and assistance on how to score the next victory against the next adversary - then, the victory will have *increased* his power. If a sustaining a loss, is a way to avoid being thrown out of the game completely and leads to useful (but false) perception of ones ability to put up a fight and sustain it for an extended period of time, then this victory would have led to an increase in power, since while the loser is resting, the victors would be fighting to their exhaustion, thus allowing the loser to learn important lessons, without having gone through the actual experiences.

- **The passage of time:** As time passes certain ideas, forms and structures, practices and tools, either lose their edge, or increase in their utility. If these tools, ideas and structures aren't made use of during their prime, then as the time passes, the power of its owner or practitioner decreases. Such a decrease in power might be - or might not be visible to these players. But after the age has passed, any investments made in the relics of a gone-by age, are nothing but harm to the entity itself.

Components of Power

Knowledge

- Knowledge of people, their histories, hierarchies, loyalties, partnerships or relationships; strengths and weaknesses; educational level, personality, etc...
- Knowledge of the relevant organizations and institutions, their history; the rules and principles based on which they operate, and based of which they judge; the standards, the communication protocols; the emergency procedures or protocols, the organizations resources; its strengths and weaknesses; its friends and foes etc...
- Knowledge of the processes, tools and techniques, locations, information systems etc...

Communication

- Communication of purpose, values, culture, norms, attitudes, emotions, experiences etc...
- Communication of threats, opportunities, the state of the organization or entity other changes in the environment etc...
- Communication of needs, wants, intentions, plans, tools and techniques, methods, technologies etc...

Alliances

- Alliances built on mutual interests.
- Alliances built on shared values.
- Alliances built on shared values and long term mutual interests.

Automation through institutions

Institutions play a crucial role in maintaining order and preventing chaos. Those entities who fail to establish, finance, improve and capitalize on the strengths of their and others' would have failed to automate those crucial tasks that tend to require a great deal of attention to detail, *if* they aren't managed by specialist organizations. Entities or players, have to find a way to automate such tasks as, the production of new knowledge, the maintaining and expansion of the transactional relationships, the detection of threats to its well being and so forth. These tasks can be automated through effective institutions, who are equipped to perform these tasks under various constraints. By automation I mean a combination of standardization, simplification, classification, detection, analysis, outsourcing, quantification (mathematization), and computerization of tasks; threats and opportunities, and changes in the environment. The more automated the tasks and processes of the given players, the more powerful and resilient the player is relative to other players.

Projection of Power

The successful projection of power is all about understanding the relationships between the different components of power, and the various environmental variables. It is about understanding and making the right choice of actions, the right choice of timing of those actions, and the right choice of tools and techniques. Here, the leader of the organization or the individual players themselves will shine the most, since the projection of power has a great deal to do with the personality, experiences, and upbringing of the leaders themselves. An intelligent, ruthless *yet* humble leader will leave a very different impression on the various friendly and adversarial players of the game, compared to an intelligent, ruthless *and* megalomaniac leader. Power in its purest form, is nothing more then a static tool. The temperament and creativity of the user will determine what *can* be - and what *will* be achieved with it. The worst kind of leaders in such a situation, that one can come across, are the easily excited ones. These are the impulsive ones. The second worse are the indecisive ones; These are usually individuals beyond their forties, who have not acquired the necessary amount of experience with uncertainty, during their life, and cannot engage in the quick calculations (involving sacrifice and compromise), that leadership requires at times. The third worse are the deaf ones, whom people find it hard to get them to consider alternative courses of actions, and these are usually the foolish ones. The longer such leaders are in charge, the faster the power projection ability of the organization is going to diminish.

The Choice of Action

- Military
- Political
- Judiciary
- Intelligence / Covert
- Financial / Economic / Business
- Social / Psychological / Anthropological
- Pedagogical / Educational
- Environmental
- Technological / Scientific / Informational / Computational

The Choice of Timing

It is a cliche, but it still begs mentioning, *timing is everything.* For example: for a politician to say things during the election, will have a very different effect on his power status - then if he had said the same thing before, or after the election. For a general to go on the offensive before the enemy has assembled in order - is going to have a drastically different effect on the outcome of the battle (and perhaps the war), then if he had made his move, while the enemy was still in disarray. Almost all mistakes can be considered mistakes of timing. The study of power projection, and that of victory *has to be,* and inadvertently *is* a study of timing.

A WORD ON POWER, AND ITS PROJECTION

The Choice of Tools and Techniques

Each type of action has its plethora of tools and techniques. The same action, performed with the same timing, but with different tools and techniques can, and will often times lead to drastically different results. Here the judgment of the player is the ultimate determining factor of the future power dynamics of the game.

These together, with the given context in which the decision makers are operating, will determine the scope of the action, its potency, and its effects on the organization acting, and the environment being acted on (as it is constantly changing).

II

PART TWO: DESIGNING FOR SUPREMACY, NOT SURVIVAL

The Muslim's Handbook itself is designed to serve as a field manual for all decision makers, regardless of their circumstances and/or educational level. This part of the book will provide practical guidance on how we can outwit the devil, and score a lasting victory in our struggles for supremacy.

Each chapter starts with some introductory remarks, and ends with What we can do section which presents the practical steps we can take to improve our circumstances.

5

The Identity, Values And Symbolism Of The Ummah

All our efforts, aims, means and relationships must be informed by the Prophetic Tradition of the prophets of Allah, as they are mentioned in the Quran and the Sunnah. Before embarking on any struggle - we have to make sure, that our plans, and attitudes are not devoid of the *barakah*, that Allah has made available to the Believers. All our efforts must be informed by the identity and values of this Ummah, as they were understood and embodied by the first three generations of Muslims. Those values, attitudes, symbols, verbal and literary expressions, questions, methodologies, modes of behavior and mannerisms, frames of thinking and points of reference - that are not in line with that of our *Pious Predecessors* - are not for our benefit, but for our destruction and misguidance. And we ask Allah, Exalted Be He, to grant us the strength to stand by the principles with which He elevated the disgraceful Arabs, to the enduring and lofty examples of great morals, and just conduct.

It is necessary that we Muslims remind ourselves of that extraordinary legacy of all of the Prophets and Messengers of Allah - that *we* carry on our shoulders. Yes, we have over one thousand four hundred years of history to look up to, and we are obligated to use it as a lens to look at the world. The past two hundred years of propaganda against Islam and Muslims - and most especially the attitudes of the world since 9/11, makes this a necessary step in order to address our inner needs, before we address our material needs.

This chapter is designed to aid us in this crucial task of introspection.

The Traits of a Muslim and the Practices That Define Us

To simplify the task of introspection, we can look at the embodiment of our values and attitudes, and the practices of our father Ibrahim, peace be upon him. He is a bright example of what we Muslims ought to embody. Our identity, values and practices aren't informed by our desires and opinions (based on those desires), but rather they are those values with which Allah Has described us / prescribed for us - and blessed us with, in the Quran.

> **Strive for ⌈the cause of⌉ Allah in the way He deserves, for ⌈it is⌉ He ⌈Who⌉ has *chosen* you, and laid upon you no hardship in the religion—the way of your forefather Abraham. ⌈It is He (Allah) Who named you 'Muslims' ⌈in the⌉ earlier ⌈Scriptures⌉ and in this ⌈Quran⌉, so that the Messenger may be a witness over you, and that you may be witnesses over humanity. So establish prayer, pay alms-tax, and hold fast to Allah. He ⌈alone⌉ is your Guardian. What an excellent Guardian, and what an excellent Helper!** Quran 22:78

The following are the traits, attributes and practices of our father Ibrahim (peace be upon him).

- **Devotion and Submission to Allah:** being dedicated to the cause of Allah, being available for His call whenever He calls. Those orders that Allah gives, are being welcomed with pleasure as good news, and acted upon with uninterrupted focus and His Policies implemented with undisturbed puritanism. Our father Ibrahim was always oriented towards those goals that Allah set for him, and with unshakable optimism and faith in the promise of Allah. That is the legacy which we have to look up to.

When his Lord said to him, "Submit," he said, "I have submitted [in Islām] to the Lord of the worlds." Quran 2:131

Indeed, Abraham was a model of excellence: devoted to Allah, ⌈perfectly⌉ upright—not a polytheist. Quran 16:120

...by men who are not distracted—either by buying or selling—from Allah's remembrance, or performing prayer, or paying alms-tax. They fear a Day when hearts and eyes will tremble. Quran 24:37

- **Independence:** of action and always taking the initiative. Not waiting for some Messiah figure to appear and take charge. Rather, constantly acknowledging the omnipresence of The Creator of all the Worlds, and that He is always with those who believe and carry His Banner. The servant-master relationship between us Muslims and our Master, Allah — leaves no room for mere mortals (especially non-Muslims) to introduce constraints, or guidelines to the fulfillment of our vows, promises and duties to our Master. Thus, a Muslim doesn't need anyone's permission or approval to do the right thing, at the ideal time and place, with the necessary and useful tools. Once it has become clear, what is pleasing and displeasing to Allah, Muslims will (have to) take actions as a community, well organized and managed - and as individuals, if the community is too weary of making the right decisions.

And [mention, O Muḥammad], when Abraham said to his father and his people, "Indeed, I am disassociated from that which you worship". Quran 43:26

- **Reliance on Allah**

That is because Allâh is the Maulâ (Lord, Master, Helper, Protector, etc.) of those who believe, and the disbelievers have no Maulâ (lord, master, helper, protector, etc.). Quran 47:11

- **Selflessness and Generosity**

Indeed, Allah has purchased from the believers their lives and their properties [in exchange] for that they will have Paradise. They fight in the cause of Allah, so they kill and are killed. [It is] a true promise [binding] upon Him in the Torah and the Gospel and the Qur'ān. And who is truer to his covenant than Allah? So rejoice in your transaction which you have contracted. And it is that which is the great attainment. Quran 9:111

Then after the fear had left Abraham, and the good news had reached him, he began to plead with Us for the people of Lot. Quran 11:74

- **Courage:** and the will to sacrifice, and confront difficulties in the path of Allah. And taking the initiative to undo evil, rather then wait for evil to establish its strongholds in the minds and hearts of people.

> **Those to whom people [i.e., hypocrites] said, "Indeed, the people have gathered against you, so fear them." But it [merely] increased them [the believers] in faith, and they said, "Sufficient for us is Allah, and [He is] the best Disposer of affairs."** Quran 3:173

- **Walaa wal Baraa and Protective Gheera (Jealousy).**

> **You already have an excellent example in Abraham and those with him, when they said to their people, "We totally dissociate ourselves from you and ⌈shun⌉ whatever ⌈idols⌉ you worship besides Allah. We reject you. The enmity and hatred that has arisen between us and you, will last until you believe in Allah alone." The only exception is when Abraham said to his father, "I will seek forgiveness for you,⌉" adding, "but⌉ I cannot protect you from Allah at all." ⌈The believers prayed,⌉ "Our Lord! In You we trust. And to You we ⌈always⌉ turn. And to You is the final return.** Quran 60:40

> **and ⌈that of⌉ Abraham, who ⌈perfectly⌉ fulfilled ⌈his covenant⌉?** Quran 53:37

- **Long Term Thinking:** We Muslims aren't just concerned with our own temporary desires and wishes, but rather the long term well being of human beings. And we are not just concerned with needs of human beings in this world, but also their well being in their graves, and the Hereafter.

> **And who is better in religion than one who submits himself to Allah while being a doer of good and follows the religion of Abraham, inclining toward truth? And Allah took Abraham as an intimate friend.** Quran 4: 125

These are the traits of Muslims and these are the practices that define us. And no matter how far away Muslims stray away from The Path of Allah, they are still closer to it then the Kuffar. And no matter how much effort the Kuffar exert in acquiring these attributes and virtues, they will never come to embody them except through Islam, and Islam alone.

Those ambitious Muslim leaders who fail to instill, strengthen and capitalize on these attributes of Muslims, are not the leaders of Muslims. These are the attributes that bring people closer to Allah. And those people who distance us from these traits are our clear adversaries. Those processes and ideas that keep us away from such virtuous practices are destructive and terrible schemes, that have to be met with uncompromising opposition.

Those Muslims who wish to be leaders of Muslims must study these attributes of the Prophet and his companions, and learn how to instill these in others - and once they have become known for that, they will naturally be raised to positions of leadership — *as* they would have deserved to be raised.

The Objection of the Kuffar

The Kuffar wonder, why are Muslims so sensitive and thin skinned regarding their Prophet and their Holy Book. How is it, they wonder - that just by seeing a bunch of papers (The Quran) being burned, they get triggered and start rioting. And they further give examples and comparisons; of the burning of the books of other religious groups, say Jews, Hindus and Christians. Why are The Holy Book and Prophet of the Muslims to receive special respect and consideration, when the Books of The Christians, Jews, Hindus and other religious groups, have been made fun of for much longer? Such are the misunderstandings of Islam on the part of the non-Muslims, who *choose* not learn, but still wish to pass judgment. Misunderstandings about what the Quran means, symbolizes and represents to Muslims. Since most attempts made so far to educate the Kuffar about how Muslims see the world, have proven ineffective in remedying this ignorance — I think a simpler language is in order. The ideas and symbols of Islam can perhaps best be explained through analogies with the attitudes and symbols that are familiar to non-Muslims. And not that there is anything analogous in the symbols of non-Muslims, to the symbols of Muslims - but the mere act of putting things in the greater context should yield the necessary insight that would help the non-Muslims understand the status of The Holy Quran and of The Noble Prophet Muhammad, peace and blessings be upon him. The following is one such example.

Imagine some Muslim takes a western (say, French) flag, book of law, constitution, passport and the statues of important figures – the heroes of that nation and the culturally important works of art – and he throws dung at them, sprays them with the blood of a pig, and then lights all of that on fire. And lets assume that it is known, that the purpose with which he is doing that, is to get under the skin of the non-Muslims.

How would – for example, the French react? Will they be able to bear that with patience and prevent themselves from reactionary behavior? Will they calm down each other by reminding themselves, that the things that were abused weren't anything more then just some fabric, paper and stones/metal (the statues). Or will they be quick to realize, that what is being communicated through this act, is the hatred and disgust of this group (Muslims) – towards these symbols and all that they represent? And wouldn't the more experienced thinkers among non-Muslims derive from such a behavior an intention, and a desire on the part of these Muslims, to burn and destroy all those institutions, ideas and peoples that hold these Western ways of life, beliefs and symbols dear and sacred?

They (non-Muslims) *most definitely* would react with anger and fury. But if they didn't – that would also be understandable, given the fact that self-respect has become quite a foreign thing to the Western man. The only creed that he defines himself by after all, is *capital*.

The Quran, the Kuffar must understand - is our constitution, our book of law, our flag, our anthem, our defender, our witness, our prosecutor and our judge — *and* a thousand times more then that. Unlike the ever-changing flimsy 'values', symbols, constitutions, laws, attitudes and philosophies of the non-Muslims', the Holy Quran has been the Muslims' identity, arbiter and guide for more then one thousand years. For the Kuffar to not appreciate the enduring power of the Book of Allah and consider it equal to their own books of law that they write, and rewrite with their own hands, is one serious crime. The non-Muslims are attacking Muslims, when they disrespect the Quran, because the Quran is the only thing by which we define, and differentiate ourselves from the rest of the religious and non-religious communities and groups. The Quran is the Muslims' **identity!**

This is the difference between the Quran and all of the rest of the books, practices, creeds and symbols by which non-Muslims define themselves. And perhaps this example would be sufficient to enlighten non-Muslims – as to the significance of the Quran. Its value is not what you (the non-Muslims) give it. Its value is that, which Muslims have given it, and greater.

For those who wish to understand the status of the Holy Quran, it would be sufficient to consider the fact that this book is the only reason we Muslims have not treated the disbelievers with as much injustice, and hatred as they have treated Muslims or their fellow non-Muslims. If it wasn't for the Muslims' reverence for the Quran, Muslims would have brought on the non-Muslim world, nothing short of that which the Western non-Muslims brought about on each other through the Napoleonic and World Wars, and the Colonial nightmares to which they subjected the rest of the world for centuries. Non-Muslims must appreciate the fact, that if it weren't for this book, we 'terrorists and barbarians' would have surely treated the Kuffar in an equally amoral fashion.

Perhaps the Kuffar will soon realize that it is this very book, because of which Muslims have been behaving and living according to the 'Meccan Period', and if it wasn't for this book, Muslims would have been walking around always, everywhere with attitudes of the 'Medinan Period'. **And** Muslims must realize, that if they do not start treating the Kuffar in accordance with the Medinan attitudes - the Kuffar will never stop treating us according to the Meccan attitudes.

The fact that the Westerners judge Islam and Muslims build off of the assumptions of western societies, cultures, attitudes and 'values'— should be sufficient for people to understand, that the image of Islam, it's symbols and it's adherents that filters out through this lens is perverted. Most, if not all of Westerns assumptions, as it pertains to Islam and Islamic societies, do not hold true.

Below are some practical steps we Muslims can take to remedy our identity related problems. And in the process undo the demonic influences that some Muslim and *many* non-Muslim elite have been exercising on our affairs. All these ideas, have to be seen in the context of the other ideas and strategies mentioned in this book.

What We Muslims Can Do, to Better Assert Our Identity, Values and Practices

- People should avoid using, or accepting the use, and adoption of labels that might have religious or sectarian connotation to them, or the potential for one in the long run (e.g. Deobandi, al Azhari). Those Muslims, and specifically students of knowledge who wish to distinguish themselves by such labels, and flaunt unnecessary titles, also bear responsibility for the rising divisiveness in the Ummah. Instead what they should do, is try to have as much similarity between themselves and the Sahaba, the Tabi'uun and their students. Allah named us "Muslims", *not* Deobandis and Azharis.

- Community leaders, du'at and students of knowledge must always be on the watch for undesirable phenomenon from taking hold in the communities and the Ummah at large. Among the worst of these phenomenon is the formation of personality cults around influential and/or charismatic individuals (e.g. Rabee' Ibn Hadi Al Madkhali).

- For the Muslim youth, the first and most important thing to do, is to become independent - socially, emotionally and financially. This way others (especially their elders) won't be able to exercise much authority on them - especially the toxic manipulation that some youth are put through as it relates to marriage, career choice and the practicing of religion. It is primarily the psychological and/or financial dependence of the victims, and their quietness often times that allows for such abuse to arise and continue (which shouldn't be interpreted as victim blaming). This kind of psychological, and social dependence on other people goes against the traits of our father Ibrahim specifically, and all of the other prophets of Allah more generally. It is this dependence of the innocent youth on the shameless manipulators that has led to the withering of much talent, dreams and decisive action, and plans for strengthening the Ummah and weakening it's antagonists.

- Muslims, especially our community leaders and du'at must stop self-censoring. People in the Ummah who are well versed in media studies, and have a strong personality - and have mastered rhetorical tactics, should be given the responsibility of presenting Islam, and representing Muslims on local and global platforms — not those who have only inquired into religious sciences through Western academia, have no militancy, and have no useful understanding of applied social sciences. The Muslim community and institutions must have specially trained media-aware people to engage with the media and the world at large. If we Muslims continue self-censoring, we Muslims continue being the cause of our own demise and the cause of the exponentially increasing corruption across the world. We have the ability and religious obligation to embody and act according to the attributes of our father Ibrahim (may peace be upon him). We have the responsibility and duty to stop the world from going to the extremes - the way it has been going ever since Muslims became too worldly (and thus weak) - over a century ago.

- Muslims must be puritanical, even against themselves. Indeed the worst punishments and harshness that anyone should ever receive from us, because of their crimes - are those nearest and dearest to us. The nepotism among Muslims and the defense, and protection of corrupt people or criminals (often times our own relatives and friends), has been one of the main causes of the Ummah's fragility and disunity.

> **Say, [O Muḥammad], "If your fathers, your sons, your brothers, your wives, your relatives, wealth which you have obtained, commerce wherein you fear decline, and dwellings with which you are pleased are more beloved to you than Allah and His Messenger and jihād [i.e., striving] in His cause, then wait until Allah executes His command. And Allah does not guide the defiantly disobedient people." Quran 9:24**

- Those buildings, institutions, roads, prizes, medals, chairs of honor, and statues that are named after or built in honor of the religious innovators, extremists, corrupt and/or incompetent politicians, immoral and/or hedonistic artists, should be renamed after the competent, conscientious, and pious people of the past. Naming things in honor of living individuals should be avoided.

> **Then is the one who laid the foundation of his building on righteousness [with fear] from Allah and [seeking] His approval better, or the one who laid the foundation of his building on the edge of a bank about to collapse, so it collapsed with him into the fire of Hell? And Allah does not guide the wrongdoing people. Quran 9:109**

- Those posters, paintings, pictures of political leaders in governmental offices, on bill boards, street walls and buildings should be replaced with appropriate Islamic art that strengthen the spirit of Muslims, and raises the ambitions of the viewers to compete in goodness and in service to Islam, Muslims and humanity at large.

- Muslims should stop writing, shouting, singing and protesting in support of immoral principles and ways of life (e.g. LGBTQ+). This is *not* what our Prophet and his companions sacrificed their lives for. This is not what they fought for on empty stomachs, and in scorching heat. If we continue down this path, with our heads hanging down in self-pity, the punishment of Allah won't be delayed for much longer. The truth is scary indeed. Most Muslims are but a hair width away from kufr and nifaaq. We are way too busy trying to please humans, when Allah is much more deserving that we should please Him, by affirming all that He gave to His Prophet, including that which displeases the disbelievers - and taking pride in those things that distinguish us, and our way of life, from the Kuffar.

- All that can be Islamized, should be Islamized for the benefit of the Muslims so that no entity or organization of any kind can gain the upper hand on Muslims, and so that we may be independent of non-Muslims (e.g. The Islamization of logic was an extraordinary boost to Islamic intellectuals who before that had a loophole in their defenses and weaknesses in their offenses against the different people of desires, and of religious innovators).

- We Muslims must investigate, understand and acknowledge the demonic efforts, schemes, and campaigns against our identity, sovereignty and most importantly our core mission – spreading The Word of Allah to all the civilizations (human and other intelligent species) that we have, and *may* come across.

Alif, Lām, Rā. [This is] a Book which We have revealed to you, [O Muḥammad], that you might bring mankind out of darknesses into the light by permission of their Lord - to the path of the Exalted in Might, the Praiseworthy. Quran 14:1

- A Renaissance requires renaissance men and women. We don't make our decisions based on how much we like the choices/options. But rather based on how much the Ummah and Humanity are in need of it. Based on how quickly it will bring us closer to the Islamic Ideals. The same applies when it comes to making the big decisions of life – especially choosing a career. Thus, Muslims have to abandon their obsessions with their own desires and wishes that do not serve Islam. What Muslims are most in need of today, are polymaths who have strong personalities, and resolute allegiance to Islam and Muslims - and are in vehement opposition to kufr and Kuffar. Muslims, who are already experts in one field, should explore the sciences, arts and trades beyond their current expertise. There are solutions, strategies, ideas, patterns, problems, arguments, questions, answers and tools, and techniques that are not visible *except* to the masters of multiple trades. We have plenty of experts, and all praises belong to Allah for that - what we lack, are experts who can serve as guides and leaders to other experts. These are the polymaths that we have to have, if we are to undo the demonic schemes against Islam and Humanity.

Say, "Indeed, my prayer, my rites of sacrifice, my living and my dying are for Allah, Lord of the worlds.". Quran 6:162

6

Education

The best warranty and security against any disaster is a well educated, well thought, well connected, and well traveled population. This has been one of the main motivations for the authoring of this book. The success of our strategy as an Ummah, will be measured, monitored, and evaluated based on how connected, educated, sophisticated, cultured and traveled the average Muslim becomes with the passage of time. And based on how connected, organized, automated, secured and resourceful our organizations become. To obtain all of these results, and quickly - we need experts. This chapter focuses on the techniques, strategies and technologies that we can employ to achieve our goals without much sweating.

The immediate industrialization of the Muslim World demands that the technical education of the population, and workers - across industries and organizations, be practical and pragmatic, and not theoretical and computational, where the student has no way of connecting the theory to the actual practices of/in industry and/or domestic hobby.

The industrial revolutions of the past were not headed by highly educated abstract thinkers, but rather by pragmatic visionaries (Commodore Vanderbilt, Thomas Edison, John D. Rockefeller, Matsushita Konosuke, Henry Ford etc...). Nor were the employees working in their factories serious engineers with mathematical backgrounds or understanding of the complete engineering cycle of researching, planning, designing, prototyping, testing and mass assembling. Most of the workers didn't even have something that would be considered the equivalent of a high school diploma, or indeed even middle school level education. And yet, the West and to an extent the East, still saw industrialization of an unfathomable scale and scope.

Thus, if we are to kick start a process of rapid industrialization, we must let people play to their strength, and not demand or expect – or indeed, *accept* that high school diploma be a requirement for working in factories. A great deal more can be said about the ingredients of successful industrialization. But it won't be necessary or befitting in this book, as our main focus is on prescriptions, and not descriptions and analysis.

This chapter addresses the various changes that we can make in our educational systems and practices, to speed up the improvement process. Thus, achieving in months, In Shaa Allah - that which we haven't been able to achieve in decades - both on a personal level as individuals, and on an organizational and institutional level.

The Requirements That Our Educational Systems, Institutions, Practices, Materials and Policies Should Meet

- The time of producing experts has to be decreased (to less then 8 years - as measured from the first day the student steps into a school, not knowing anything - to the day when s/he is graduates as an expert).

- The need for competent, expert teachers of the respective fields has to be decreased.

- The education/learning must be independent of any physical location, and not have specified (strict) time constraints.

- The success of the educational system should not be dependent on, - or affected by the short-term economic, financial or political circumstances and/or fluctuations of the country.

- The learning process must afford everyone the independence to learn at their own pace, such that the gifted students won't get bored with the repetition of what they have already understood and mastered, and the challenged students won't feel hopeless (as a result of group pressure, or a sense of having to always catch up to others, because they might take longer to understand and appreciate certain concepts). No student is bound by the progress of the other students. Rather everyone is moving independently on which ever path they choose for themselves. This would increase competition among the students. And maybe they should be able to see each others' performance (thus gamefying all learning) for greater motivation.

- The educational resources, opportunities and avenues must be equal for people of all ages, genders, races etc…

How a Novice Becomes an Expert

Because we have limited ourselves in this book to answering the question of, what we *can* do, I have not explored the crucial topic of *how a novice becomes an expert*. I will leave this topic for the readers to explore on their own.

Find out, *how* a novice becomes an expert. You can refer to the book mentioned below.

How Learning Happens: Seminal Works in Educational Psychology and What They Mean in Practice. Authors: Paul A. Kirschner, Carl Hendrick; Illustrated by Oliver Caviglioli

What We Can Do

Education of Technical Fields

- The universities and high schools must *adopt* the latest and greatest tools in mathematics, and other stem fields. One of these is Clifford/Geometric Algebra, which would replace your typical linear algebra, tensors and other ideas that are way to varied and complicated and time consuming.

- The textbooks on science and engineering should be written using Clifford Algebra.

- The teaching of linear algebra, calculus, differential equations, probability and statistics to children must be normalized. They needn't understand the derivations, or be able to carry out all of the computations — rather, they would focus on the conceptual underpinnings of the theorems, understand where they are useful through practical examples, images, animations etc... And be able to formulate real world problems in mathematical notation, *and* solve the equations using computers. The actual task of computation must at no point be done by the student, as that is just not how things are done in the real world. They must understand, and be able to explain things like the different types of differential equations, linear transformations, various theorems etc... As they learn to use the theorems in an appropriate manner, they would be slowly introduced to the derivations and proofs. (**Concepts - Relevance - Application - Practice - Contextualization - Practice - Derivations - Practice**).

- The education of healthcare fields in developing countries must be begin with very specialized curriculum: e.g: dentistry: Some students start with learning and practicing tooth cleaning from the very beginning, other students in the taking of tooth, while others in something else, and each university has its hospital, where you get virtually free healthcare.

- The industrial workers should be given a hands-on training related to industrial processes, manufacturing technologies, machinery (and machine elements), tools, organizational / project / operational management.

- Schools of languages, and diplomacy have to be established where current, and future diplomats receive training on the finer points of the social sciences to deal with the current, and future challenges facing the nation. The schools are also supposed to be filters for finding the most talented, and hardworking people for different positions in the government, military and business world.

Children's Education

- All schools including kindergartens should be led/principled by people with PhD's in some field - if for no other reason, then to make sure that the people who are responsible for our educational institutions are the most hyper conscientious people that the society has to offer.

- Children must learn project management, accounting and finance, already in the first grade. And that knowledge should be emphasized in every grade, until by the age of 15, the children have a perfect understanding of project management and project portfolio management.

- Instead of subjecting children to 12 years of general education. They could be thought through nano/micro degree programs, each one focusing on individual skills and lasting 6 – 9 months. After students have studied four grades worth of material, they should start specializing. The educational system should emphasize the strengths and interests of the learner.

- Children must learn practical, fundamental and necessary skills, that they will be needing in the real world, once they grow up. The learning of such practical skills will motivate the students, since they are able to see the immediate fruits of his/her struggles, through the greater and deeper comprehension of their environment and a higher self-efficacy when it comes to survival and prospering in the real world. This is - and Allah knows best, the key to making people life-long learners. Some of these skills are: self-teaching, touch typing, critical thinking, logic, mathematical proofs, leadership, logistics, swimming, martial arts, writing, negotiating, project management, bookkeeping / accounting; personal and international finance / trade / economics - all to an extent, that they will be able to understand the most common financial data and reports / news; statistical thinking, system thinking, programming, algorithmic thinking, decision making, A few things about cryptography, and Arabic fluency etc…

Learning Platforms, Institutions and Practices

- All learning material from the alphabet to the most advanced subjects in STEM fields and social sciences must be put into a digital platform in at least one language - that is Arabic. The learning platform is interactive, and monitored by the education ministries of the Muslim World. There is no real concept of classes/standards, but rather anyone can study any subject, to any extent that he/she pleases - and then takes the test which is automatically graded, and if successful gets a certificate. The certificate is/should be valid across the Muslim World. There are however certain subjects/topic/sections that all students must study/memorize. The platform must be designed such that it is constantly trying to improve the pattern recognition skills of the student. Also, all of the learning material must be revised on regular intervals, to make sure that the students don't forget what they have already learned. Such a platform will eliminate the need for a knowledgeable teacher. And the teacher himself can be some university student who is in charge of the learning room for a week. Each university student has to accumulate at least one, or two weeks of teaching/monitoring experience per year of study. The class tables in school, could be a big screen, where the educational software is installed. Each student would get an RFID card specific to them, with which only they can access their account. All of the labs can/should be incorporated into the platform. So the software must have a virtual chemical Lab, electronics design and simulation lab, 3D design and simulation lab etc…

- All of the certificates that students earn are saved in the system, and is saved with the ministry of education.

- Universities must become much more connected with the business world so that students are always getting a good glance at the real world.

- Since the students coming to university would have already learned the different ways of thinking, and have been constantly applying them - there would be no need for them to take 'general knowledge' courses in the university. The university curricula should be designed such that, within a year of studying you would be an expert in the given field. But of course, everyone is allowed to move in their own pace.

- Standardize the tools and processes of/or related to education e.g. instead of every Islamic country producing its own digital learning platforms, we can build one excellent platform, in which all of the learning material is available in all of those languages that Muslims speak. This would reduce the fragility of our educational systems. The platform isn't just managed by one country, but rather by ALL Muslim countries. If one nation becomes weak, and cannot maintain the educational infrastructure, that wouldn't affect their population, since the same educational service is maintained, and offered for free by the rest of the Muslim World. It is such distributed systems that we must design, if we are to rapidly recover from our weaknesses.

- Science hubs: a place where free resources are provided to students to build new devices (electronic, mechanical and chemical). All electronics components, different chemicals with a good safety profile, circuit boards (and their machines), computers for designing stuff, 3d printers. Science hubs and libraries could/should be open 24/7.

- Building libraries in all places with inspiring Islamic books for children and adults, various kinds of books on science and engineering, computers where students can learn and practice different skills in virtual environments, including with the help of *genuinely* fun games.

- A portion of the Ummah has to always be in the domain of the 'impossible', 'the unknown', the extremely difficult so that their intellects might become the worlds best. This is how we can produce new knowledge, and maintain the competitive advantage of the Muslim Ummah. And these researchers, u'lama and thinker should be payed handsomely.

- In order to increase the creativity of students and arouse their curiosity, and maintain their motivation - one hour in school can be dedicated to thinking creatively about inventions, problems, the future etc... The students are provided some problems about which they have to think and write down their ideas. For each problem they would write multiple solutions - which can then be discussed in groups.

Dealing With Counter Forces and Scoring a Long Term Victory:

(First read chapter 8, section: "HR Strategy of the Ummah and Managing Sensitive Projects")

Rendering the strategies of the enemies of Islam useless would require:

- Making scientific/technical knowledge widely available, through social media, video sharing services, TV channels.

- Also this knowledge should also be installed on USB sticks, hard drives DVDs, CDs and distribute around the CDs world.

- The DIY, Build-It-Yourself attitude, mentality and projects as demonstrated by others on the internet.

- these videos, content would be shown on all media services, especially on TV 24/7 over time the population itself is going to develop the intuition, and desire for producing machinery, tools for themselves.

- Successful and competent individuals who are engaged in works like manuscript editing should find themselves young, and energetic students who can learn the craft from them, and assist them in quickly bringing the forgotten / suppressed history of the Ummah to public awareness. Such important things cannot be taken lightly anymore as the world is forgetting, ignoring or ignorant to begin with, of the contributions of the Muslim Ummah to their existence, and well being. Manuscripts of all kind from the Muslim world must immediately be edited, and connected to the rest of our body of historical works. The scientific manuscripts need experts in Arabic, Farsi and Turkish and to an extent knowledge in the sciences, and mathematics. Young people must take on these responsibilities, and the older folks must take them under their wing for tutoring.

- The distribution of learning material (especially technical/scientific), DIY projects, simulations, documentaries in Micro-SD cards, USB sticks, DVD's, CD's - to people who don't have access to the internet.

- Well designed rules for intellectual property, and fast and efficient processes for bringing new technologies to markets. Connecting the inventors, and industry through standard procedures that would be known to everyone.

- All of the schools must teach something about the future. The emphasis on history is good, but we should always look forward to what kind of inventions might there be, how will the global culture change, what would the nations of the world do in the next few years, and what *should* they do; and other such questions about the future. No one knows the unseen except Allah the Lord of All Creation, but it shouldn't stop us from predicting, and teaching children how to think about the future.

- We must stop telling depressing stories, and start telling inspiring stories. Stories make up a person; if they are romanticizing ignorance, blind following, pride in un-Islamic practices and attitudes; the use of foul language towards Muslims - especially the u'lama, violence and reactionary behavior - then you can't get a person whose behavior, attitudes, mannerisms, orientation and world of ideas is Islamic. Telling the right stories, in an appropriate context, in a way that increases the confidence and pride of the Muslims, deriving relevant lessons from it - and then based on all of these, formulating practical strategies, or improving the ones that we already have to strengthen the Ummah - is an art, in which we need specialists. Everyone who reads stories, doesn't necessarily know, how to *use* the story to produce desirable results. In the beginning the least we can do is, stop telling anxiety inducing stories, and tell stories that inspire.

Further Reading

How Learning Happens: Seminal Works in Educational Psychology and What They Mean in Practice, by Paul A. Kirschner & Carl Hendrick, Illustrated by Oliver Caviglioli.

7

On Dawah and Islamic Activism

Since the turn of the millennia, Muslims have become very active in the field of dawah, which has by Allah's Grace, led to many people abandoning their hedonistic ways, and embracing the religion of Allah. At the same time however, we have seen a rise in the number of apostates. In addition to that, we have seen the Islamic World being militarily, financially and ethically attacked from all directions. We have witnessed, and are witnessing genocides of Muslims, the limitation of their religious freedoms - both in the West, and in the East, and the birth of the Islamophobia Inc - which has led to countless attacks on average Muslims in the streets, and to discrimination in organizations (including workplace discrimination, and challenges in employment). So while we have seen improvement in one area, we have witnessed inhuman decline in many other areas.

All Muslims have a role to play in improving our circumstances, and re-establishing the Ummah, as the supreme power that it once was, or even greater In Shaa Allah. To deal with these challenges, we must be realistic about all the variables that affect a civilization's or society's well being.

To begin with, let us acknowledge the fact that, people generally do not respect the weak. This is, and has been the reality of human tendencies in societies that don't have a strict criterion by which they judge across time and geography - societies that are run by emotions, in which the only ones respected and admired are those, who have something material to contribute to the lives of the masses. It is this phenomenon that is often at the roots of genocides. For us Muslims, it is different. We have lived by the Quran and the Sunnah for 1400 years. We are ordered to command good, and forbid evil - the definitions of which have not changed over time or geography. What was good in the past, is good today, and what was evil in the past, is evil today. Thus, our definitions and values are not based on the ever-changing emotions of mortal beings.

However, what happens when Muslims start bending, confusing and/or sugarcoating the rules of Islam under pressure to please the Kuffar? What happens when we *ignore* the example of our father Ibrahim, who despite being threatened with fire, and then being actually thrown into it - still did not compromise on his beliefs? What could be expected of the Kuffar, if Muslims themselves do not stand by their own religion and hold strongly to the Islamic ideals, and show eagerness to compromise on their beliefs - even when the compromise is unnecessary?

The answer to all these questions is, ***our present reality.***

In this chapter we will explore strategies for restoring the true monotheism, that our Beloved, peace and blessings be on him, was raised to preach.

> **Go forth, whether light or heavy, and strive with your wealth and your lives in the cause of Allah. That is better for you, if you only knew.** Quran 9:41

And if We had willed, We could have elevated him thereby, but he adhered [instead] to the earth and followed his own desire. So his example is like that of the dog: if you chase him, he pants, or if you leave him, he [still] pants. That is the example of the people who denied Our signs. So relate the stories that perhaps they will give thought. Quran 7:176

It is He who has sent His Messenger with Guidance and the Religion of truth (pure monotheism) to manifest it over all religion (all ways of life, all -*isms*, all methodologies, mindsets and cultures), although they who associate others with Allah dislike it. Quran 9:33

What We Can Do

The Basics

- Those Muslim men who have married women from faiths other then the Abrahamic faiths, must either annul their marriage, or request the women convert to one of the three Abrahamic faiths.

- And those Muslim women who have taken non-Muslims as their men should know that their "marriage" was never a marriage in the sight of Allah. They must request their "husband" to convert to Islam, or leave the man to start a new chapter.

- And those Muslims that are in illicit relationships should leave them.

> **Say, ⌐O Prophet, that Allah says,¬ "O My servants who have exceeded the limits against their souls! Do not lose hope in Allah's mercy, for Allah certainly forgives all sins.¹ He is indeed the All-Forgiving, Most Merciful.** Quran 39:53

- The older generation has to do everything to enable the youth to fulfill their duties. The older people must dedicate a few years of their life to the education, training, tutoring and recruitment of the conscientious and talented youth, and to help them perform their duties, and goal of transforming the Ummah for the better.

> **Say ⌐O Prophet, that Allah says¬, "O My servants who believe! Be mindful of your Lord. Those who do good in this world will have a good reward. And Allah's earth is spacious. Only those who endure patiently will be given their reward without limit."** Quran 39:10

- The youth's job it is to seize the New Era, and assert the Ummah's sovereignty. We must champion our own cause and be the leaders of our own revolution, rather then wait like fools, for the Kuffar to be our saviors, and build us a *khilafa* on the strong foundation of faith - which they don't have, nor will they ever have it, except through Islam and Muhammad. The youth must carry the flag of our religion. The Muslim youth must realize their power, and supremacy over the youth of all other faiths and ways of life. The Muslim youth must shoulder their responsibilities, and realize what abilities, and strengths Allah has blessed them with. Our youth are the ones, who will In Shaa Allah change the course of history for the whole of mankind. And the youth must march towards those great victories, prizes and adventures awaiting them in the path of Allah by following in the footsteps, and legacy of the Sahaba, may Allah be pleased with them all.

If you disbelieve, then ⌐know that¬ Allah is truly not in need of you, nor does He approve of disbelief from His servants. But if you become grateful ⌐through faith¬, He will appreciate that from you. No soul burdened with sin will bear the burden of another. Then to your Lord is your return, and He will inform you of what you used to do. He certainly knows best what is ⌐hidden¬ in the heart. Quran 39:7

Can ⌐the misguided be like¬ those whose hearts Allah has opened to Islam, so they are enlightened by their Lord? So woe to those whose hearts are hardened at the remembrance of Allah! It is they who are clearly astray. Quran 39:22

- The auxiliary sciences (u'lum ul aala) should be thought with the aid of mind maps, flow charts, Venn diagrams and other diagrams. This would make it easier for students to learn and memorize the concepts, and they would be more motivated and attracted to study.

- The du'at, students of knowledge and scholars must realize, that you don't need to answer every question that is posed to you. You don't need to give an interview every time you are asked for it. You don't need to comment on every issue and event, about which people might inquire. You don't need to denounce every 'terrorist attack' or crime committed by a Muslim. What Islam *is* and *is not,* are questions that have been addressed a million times in writing, in speech and in action. Those who wish to vilify Islam and Muslims, are going to do it, regardless of whether you are able to explain Islam's position once more, or not.

- The du'at must improve their dawah style. Instead of coming across as if they are begging people to convert to Islam, they must become, and act more confident and always have the pride of their religion, and way of life visible on their faces, and in the way they carry themselves, and in their choice of words, analogies, aphorisms, quotes, stories and questions. And most importantly, this includes preaching the complete message of Islam, without sugarcoating those things that (might) displease the disbelievers. The lack of pride in Jihad, and martyrdom that Muslims in non-Muslim majority countries demonstrate - is one pathetic aspect of our communities, which the first generations of Muslims would have punished us for. We cannot afford to sugarcoat or 'justify' or 'explain' the practices, and attitudes of the early Muslims to please the Kuffar, or to at least not anger them! or worse distort and sugarcoat the message of Islam. But if we keep sugarcoating, we are just betraying ourselves, **and** the very cause that we pretend to be supporting. If that isn't hypocrisy, then one wonders, *what is?*

- Those people who have not studied usul ul fiqh and qawa'ed ul fiqh, should not be allowed to engage in refutation of people of knowledge and/or the evaluation of u'lama, or engage in live and/or major debates. These matters have to be left to the ones who have strong foundational knowledge of all Islamic sciences, and who are well trained in rhetoric, the oratory arts, human psychology, logic and argumentation. If they are allowed, or encouraged to do so, while they might still be intellectually ill-prepared - risk turning Muslims, and Islamic sources and traditions into a plaything. The scholars must reprimand their followers and students who do so.

- The speeches given by speakers, and leaders must inspire confidence and arouse the ambition of listeners. It should make people more thoughtful, and perceptive to opportunities, especially the ones to which we are less perceptive. There is a difference between a charismatic speech, which motivates - and nervous shouting and wrangling, which leaves people confused, unmotivated and questioning. Such speech will only distance the individuals from the mosque, and makes the haram, even more seductive then it already is. Everyone who has a mouth shouldn't be allowed to give khutbah. Rather, it should be those people who are excellent rhetoricians, are well acquainted with literature of that specific culture, and have the ability to use all of the different literary devices that might prove useful. They would prepare every khutbah with mathematical precision, and throughout the week, so that when they finally deliver it on Friday, it would have the desired effect. Those imams, who cannot do the required work of writing, structuring, practicing its delivery, and upon need, rewriting the speech, or do not possess and exude the required charisma, must limit themselves to leading the prayers - the khutbah should be outsourced to someone, who has the talent and work ethic to match the responsibility.

- For maximum productivity we must establish a hierarchy, based off of which we choose which topics to talk about, which things to plan for and carry out and which things to do. For example, people living in the west, who can't influence political affairs in the Muslim world shouldn't speak about it, in short what you cannot influence you shouldn't spend your limited mental, physical and financial resources on, you shouldn't talk about it, google it, ask about it etc. Focus on what you can control. In global crisis situations, it can be transformative to move our attention to things that we can influence and control, and away from those, that are beyond our present abilities.

- Protest for what is yours, and against that, which is being unjustly forced on you, **UNTIL YOU GET WHAT YOU WANT.** This includes, protesting against the likes of PREVENT strategy; protesting for Muslim prisoners who have been unjustly imprisoned, especially the u'lama; protesting against the invasion and bombing of Muslim countries; protesting against the sanctions and economic terrorism against Muslims; protesting against the systemic surveillance and monitoring of Muslim communities in non-Muslim majority countries; protesting against the limitation of religious freedoms, in countries like France. As for exercising violence in these protests, then it is a *must*. Muslims have protested peacefully, but for every peaceful protest in non-Muslim majority countries - Muslims in their lands got nothing but bombs, thievery, assassinations and organized decapitation strikes, stripping us of our charismatic leaders and strength.

Dealing with Religious Innovations and Innovators

The Islamic institutions (especially the educational institutions) together must formulate a cohesive strategy to counter religious innovations. It should be clear to the u'lama and du'at, that religious innovations in our modern times, where they have taken on a monstrous proportion, cannot be addressed by individual effort, even if the effort is exerted everywhere, using every tool available. Rather, such endemic lack of reason among Muslim populations concerning their religious practices, has to be addressed with a cohesive long term strategy that systematically makes visible to people the schemes of the devils, by tracing the origin of the various religious innovations to the pagan rituals that they come from.

The following are some elements and steps of a practical strategy that would unite the Muslims on the Sunnah of our Beloved, may Allah's peace and blessings be on him for eternity:

- Universities such as the Islamic universities of Medina & Mecca, should offer nano-degrees to students from those nations, where religious innovations are most rampant.

- Such educational institutions should maintain a well researched list of the various religious innovations, that are prevalent in all of the Muslim communities across the globe. Each of the innovation is explored in-depth to understand its origins and relation to other religions and cults.

- And then develop an information strategy by which the Muslim populations can be informed of the faulty reasoning behind these rituals. And to warn against the unacceptable emotional attachment among Muslims to un-islamic practices. To this end, these educational institutions must assign a generous budget to the countering of religious innovations. Wealthy Muslims should provide the necessary funds to such efforts, and make sure not to miss this grand opportunity of investing with Allah, to Whom Belongs All Honor and Praise.

- The Islamic universities must further educate all aspiring leaders, scholars and influencers on the psychological warfare tactics, techniques and tools that the elite of Kuffar have been targeting Islam and Muslims with. This is perhaps the only way to ensure that Muslims are able to recognize, and distinguish the harmful from the harmless. For the children of Ibrahim and champions of Tawheed, the study of intelligence sciences is necessary, if we are to undo the manipulative efforts of the children of Iblis.

- The du'at, in addition to helping people enter into Islam, must also remain with the new Muslims, until they have fully internalized the principles of Islamic creed and the prophetic seerah, so as to prevent innovations in religion. To that end, they should have learning material, especially videos, which explain not only the technical aspects of our faith, but also compel the new Muslim to experience the journey and attitudes of the Sahaba and their Followers, by reading their history. One cannot appreciate The Guidance, that Allah has blessed them with, until they have known the sacrifices of the countless champions of this faith, may Allah be pleased with them all.

The Elite of Dawah

There has to be a special class of students of knowledge, du'at and scholars who are working on an international level; who have mastered all of the major languages (English, French, Spanish, Arabic, Urdu, Japanese, Malay, Hindi, Mandarin Chinese) and whose job it is to:

- Connect the different Muslim communities and carry the lessons from one Muslim community to another.

- Work as catalysts, networking the Muslim Ummah and making different communities aware of each others' suffering, failures, successes, strengths, opportunities, threats, resources or lack thereof etc... And helping the Muslims of one community, come to the aid of another e.g. those communities or Muslim societies that have great and experienced fighters, can help out those communities that are being threatened with genocide, or loss of their wealth and land. And those Muslim communities that have educated population can come to the aid of those communities that might not have the necessary information infrastructure to protect itself.

- Explore the communities deeply enough, to find the extremely competent, intelligent and resourceful Muslims, and then personally recruit them for various opportunities e.g. make them famous and help the rest of the Ummah to make a good use of them under various circumstances etc...

- Teach and train other du'at, in argumentation, rhetoric, public engagement, pedagogy and debating.

- Study, train and learn to recognize, analyze and counter the various satanic plans of the so-called 'International Community'. Such global and corrupt organization, have very little to do with morality, ethics or human rights – contrary to what they pretend to care about. These entities, who abhor the religion of Allah, and ignore the tears of His oppressed servants, do not serve the interests of anyone other then their founders and financiers – whose true identity should be clear to the careful observer. Indeed, they are nothing more then a bunch of cannibals in suits – hell-bent on opposing anything, that will distract from their bottom line and question their actions, plans, intentions and authority.

- Take on the responsibility of addressing the dawah weak spots (i.e. areas where there isn't the necessary amount of dawah activity) such Japan, Vietnam, China, Taiwan, Koreas, Philipines etc…

8

Human Resources, And Building Institutions

The failures of Islamic organizations, over the past two centuries, to adapt to the changing environment, and to capitalize on the opportunities offered by the new age of industrialization and information, are primarily to be attributed to a lack of organizational know-how, and/or the lack of action on this valuable knowledge. In this chapter, I have outlined a few important concepts, ideas and arguments, which I hope will serve as a reminder and guide to all Muslims, especially the ambitious ones, who aim to become influencers - and to help facilitate a must-have conversation in Muslim communities and organizations regarding the efficiency, purpose and leadership of Islamic or Muslim organizations and institutions.

On Chaos, Order and Change

Chaos – and not order, is the norm at any given time, in any given environment. To keep the chaos at bay, institutions have be to established, equipped and purposed to deal with the different forms and features of chaos. Each organization or institution has to be chipping away small chunks from the whole body of chaos and dealing with it, according to the resources available to it, and techniques and procedures, in which it has specialized. When all of the necessary institutions, with the necessary resources are present and active (as they were founded/designed to be), *order* is molded out of chaos, and uncertainty is reduced. Furthermore these organization offer means of coping with uncertainty, by facilitating communication and inter-dependent decision making.

We shouldn't be preparing for chaos, rather be preparing against it. Indeed we are not supposed to, or designed to survive chaos, rather we are designed to minimize the probability of chaos taking hold – in other words, to avoid, evade and/or mold chaos into something more benign and less debilitating. By definition, the human cognitive facilities are much more difficult to access during chaos. But people, instead of preparing against chaos are preparing *for* it - with a half-wish in the hearts some of these people, for chaos to actually befall the society, so that perhaps they can show and remind others of how the ones who didn't prepare used to ridicule all of those that did prepare for it. But preparing for chaos is actually one of the greatest causes of chaos e.g. you see people hoarding food, for a fear of food shortages, and thus causing a superficial demand which turn their claims into self-fulfilling prophesies.

Any successful social, governmental and military action requires intelligence and coordination. These two in turn, require timely communication, discipline, efficient standards and often, well defined and *just* hierarchies. When these crucial elements are denied their due attention and/or importance - organizational success is guaranteed to be at jeopardy.

Common Causes of Organizational failures are:

- Poorly trained employees or actors, including leadership: shortsightedness, inability to spot opportunities, weakness or lack of interpersonal skills, leading to an inability to establish and maintain alliances. Leaders who can't set realistic long term goals, and attach them to the day-to-day activity of the different branches of the organization; Inability to assign tasks to subordinates, and address their pedagogical needs, with the changing environment; lack of proper reward and punishment system etc.

- Lack of appropriate tools and necessary resources such as project and operational management tools, communication protocols and infrastructure, information systems, performance monitoring tools etc...

- Predatory and abusive behavior by the players within the organization (towards other actors, towards their responsibilities i.e. abusive of power, intentional misdirection and miscommunication of information); all of which results in a loss of trust - which is the single most important factor for the survival, and long term well being of any organization.

- Complacency caused by success such as when short-term successes lead to increased power plays within the organization, thus compromising the long term interests of the organization, for the immediate ego boosts of individual players.

- Unexpected / outside threats such as espionage, sabotage, assassinations, deception; unforeseen political, social, economic trends and phenomenon; natural disasters; unexpected deaths and illnesses;

Establishing Organizations

How did the Prophet establish the most successful organization that humanity has ever seen, or will ever see?

One of the major causes of failures for a major organization (such as the Ummah), is a lack of supporting organizations and institutions. The fact that an organization might have existed for a thousand years, doesn't mean that this organization has achieved its full maturity. Given the fact that, our environment is ever-changing, and sometimes in very drastic ways -we should rest assured, that no organization can succeed, unless it develops, maintains and improves strategies for the necessary change that the organization has to successfully implement, if it is to succeed. In order for us to establish or restructure and improve our organizations, we need someway of facilitating and guiding the must-have conversations. To this end, I present the readers with a checklist of organization building. The organizational leaders should contemplate over the following checklist, to get a sense of where their organization is, and where it can possibly be taken. I will let the reader ponder over the questions that we Muslims must ask, answer and discuss concerning the state of the Ummah in light of this checklist, and what needs to be done, in order to check all of the items on this list.

The organizational checklist:

- The organization's purpose.
- Physical facilities, the choice of location; digital presence, related databases and servers, data backup practices and rules.
- Responsibilities of all individuals, branches and sub-branches of the organization.
- Information infrastructure; systems, information acquisition, classification, modeling, analysis, usage, information production.
- Hierarchy and clear outline of responsibilities of each actor within the hierarchy.
- Behavioral guidelines within the organization between male/female, between junior and senior, and behavioral guidelines with outsiders etc.
- Communication protocols for intra-organizational and inter-organizational interactions; the protocols set the limits of what can be revealed etc…
- Standardized procedures for completing each task.
- Learning and training facilities, materials (documentaries, movies, simulations, animations, models, novels), tools and techniques (computational tools, Project and operational management tools, performance tracking and monitoring tools), equipment, curricula, time tables, requirements, etc.
- Recruitment strategy, process, tools and guidelines, interview questions, psychological profiling, processes for filtering away the candidates with personality problems (psychopathy, narcissism, sociopathy) etc.
- Access, authorization, security, operational security, information integrity and plans for security education, training and concern handling etc.
- Employee and stakeholder rights, responsibilities etc.
- Fraud, crime, conspiracy, piracy, distortion, espionage, sabotage - prevention, detection, notification policies and standardized procedures and tools.
- Emergency preparedness; emergency response procedures and plans,

techniques and tools, assets etc.
- Intrusion and misuse detection and prevention; security awareness and the training of the concerned parties; the development of robust countermeasures; strategies for learning from past successes and failures etc.
- Access controls, monitoring tools/policies, limitations, authorization policies.
- Organization budget, accounting, financing and checks and monitoring for suspicious activities etc.
- Organizations role, in the larger system and performance monitoring and improvement, accountability etc.
- Clearance degrees/levels that set limits on who can take part in what kinds of sensitive projects etc.
- Leadership and succession; recruitment of future operational and strategic leadership; succession policies; leadership accountability etc.

Those organizations that lack any of these points will find it difficult to handle uncertainty, even if they have all the resources.

HR Strategy of the Ummah and Managing Sensitive Projects

There is no doubt, that there are antagonists who wish us Muslims nothing, but pure evil. Muslim intellectuals, leaders from all walks of life (community leaders, tribal leaders; military, intelligence and security services leaders), scientists, engineers and gifted youth - have been systematically targeted by the enemies of Islam and Muslims. And not just individuals, but also institutions and entire countries have been destroyed by the West and the East - because of our attempts at becoming more assertive, and independent. These have included attempts at reducing our reliance on Western fiat currencies, reducing our dependence on fossil fuels by acquiring nuclear capabilities, and many other such projects that a successful nation in our modern age would aspire to have, if not need.

Our organizational leadership, structure, processes, financing, tools and techniques must be resistant against, both the well known, and lesser known tactics of sabotage, subterfuge, assassinations and other such tactics that are designed to instill fear in the hearts of Muslims (and in many cases non-Muslims who dare to defy the demons of global finance and politics).

Our tactics and strategies must be filtered through a lens of realism - *before* we start implementing them. In order for our future efforts to be successful, we must take into account the security dimension of it.

Exponentially increasing our power, and in a short time frame by connecting the different organizations, networks and communities.

Among the sources of weaknesses of the Ummah, is that the various communities of believers and institutions that we have established to strengthen our position - are not connected. By connecting the various communities of believers, and individual influencers and thinkers of the Ummah, we can quickly achieve a major breakthrough in our power status. The different minds, from different backgrounds, with different resources and strengths and weaknesses, and ideas and methodologies - when they come in contact with each other, will In Shaa Allah, lead to the flowering of countless new ideas, the implementation of strategies that might already be developed - and the strengthening of brotherly and sisterly bonds, which until now has not happened. All Muslims who are in any position to connect their brethren from one community, to believers in other communities, must do so. If the Kuffar have shown disgust towards Muslims because the believers have stood with truth, not willing to compromise for money or fame, then as these believers find each other on the truth, their resilience will increase synergistically, regardless of whether the super powers of the world stand by them or stand against them. The various communities and organizations of believers that need to be connected are:

- Virtual or cyber communities and movements
- Media organizations
- Educational organizations
- Open source communities, services and hubs
- Financial institutions
- Fundraising organizations, charities and NGOs who specialize in social work e.g. the distribution of charity to orphanages; famine; drought; flood; earth quake stricken areas
- Religious institutions
- Scientific Academia
- Military and intelligence organizations / community
- Business (service providers and industry)

9

Infrastructure And Environmental Design

Long lasting change demands that we secure the advantage of the environment, by capitalizing on those elements that improve our well being, and make us prosperous, while at the same time eliminating those elements that do us harm, such as pollutants, harmful agricultural practices and hormone disruptors.

For the Ummah to secure the advantage of the environment, we would need to rethink infrastructure, architecture, urban planning, interior design, hygiene related practices, and agricultural and industrial management, among a few other things relevant to the topic.

In this chapter, I provide some guidance and a few valuable ideas as it relates to our physical environment. Some of the topics (such as interior design) have not been addressed, and the reader is encouraged to explore them on their own. The following short section on the purpose of environmental and infrastructural upgrades, should give some hint as to what the reader should look for, while exploring further on his/her own.

The Purpose of Environmental and Infrastructural Upgrades

We have to re-imagine, redesign and restructure our environment in such a way that it:

- Helps us in our struggles, by maintaining our hope and increasing our strength and will to fight the crisis that we find ourselves in (such as, the threat and menace of global giants and their exploitation strategies and techniques - faced by both the developing and developed world etc.).
- Increases our free time which we can use for spirituality, leisure, education and self-fulfillment.
- Makes it easier for us to make healthier choices.
- Makes us feel safer, and helps us live more purposeful lives, always oriented towards the Hereafter, seeking the Face of Allah, and His Pleasure.
- Lowers the pain and burden of our responsibilities (family, workplace…), and helps us stay steadfast during trials and tribulations.
- Make our communities and the environment safer (in terms of traffic deaths etc. and crimes, such as drugs smuggling, and mass shootings etc…), more beautiful and welcoming.
- Helps us implement anti-exploitation policies and workplace rules and regulations more efficiently.
- Helps us create, provide, and maintain humane working conditions in sweatshops, factories, farmlands and industrial, political, business, security and educational organizations, offices and workplaces.

What We Can Do

Health Care

The Basics

- Screening the entire population for TB, STD's and other common infectious deceases. The victims of these deceases, should receive immediate treatment, so that they won't spread these deceases to the rest of the population. Those individuals who have incurable sexually transmitted deceases such as HIV/AIDS should be immediately eliminated, before we have any major health crisis on our hands.

- Screening the population for malnutrition, and providing the necessary financial assistance to those families. Furthermore, there should be standard nutritional aid packages for children, that could be distributed to malnourished populations.

- Addictions to drugs such as opioids and amphetamines can be cured by natural psychoactive compounds such as Ibogaine. To this end, every Muslim country (either the farmers, or the government) must allocate enough land, and resources to the cultivation of the Iboga plant, so as to meet its own needs for the anti-addiction medicine (that is Ibogaine). At the same time, efficient processes for the industrial production of this compound (and other botanical medicinal compounds), have to researched (in case such processes don't exist already) and made use of. It seems that this chemical could be the next miracle pharmaceutical, since if it is administered to entire populations of addicts, it could yield revolutionary results. There are hundreds of millions of poverty stricken people suffering from addictions, who will find such a cure to be nothing less then the undoing of a curse. While Western Big Pharma is doing all it can to destroy Western communities by the psychopathic prescriptions of addictive chemicals, Muslims must take this opportunity to recover their weaker ones from their ailments, demonstrating their enduring respect for human life.

Leisure and Recreational Infrastructure

The long-term strategy for strengthening the Ummah, has to be proactive and ambitious, not limiting Muslims to simply minimizing harm, but to also maximize happiness, at the same time not falling prey to hedonism. Islamic societies have seen a great deal of pain, and entire generations have been sustaining wound after wound. The biggest victims in these painful decades have been women. To heal these wounds, we have to direct our efforts at the mental health crisis from all angles. Recreational infrastructure is going to play as big of a role in the overall strategy for the emotional recovery of the Ummah, as financial, military and health care infrastructure. We will need to construct:

- Parks (for youth, and for families)
- Swimming pools
- Skiing resorts (both indoor and outdoor)
- Roads, off-road motorways and other necessary infrastructure for motor sports.
- Provincial / district level airfields for flying hobbyists. etc...

Most women in the poor world don't have much time for leisure and recreation, and tend to go through unbearable mental and physical health crisis. To make their lives easier, the governments and wealthy families can, for example, procure laundry machines, for however many neighborhoods they can afford, and put it at the service of the underprivileged families. Automating such physically intensive and time consuming tasks of the overworked housewives, could lead to substantial rise in their quality of life, while removing virtually nothing from the treasuries of the rich, or the governments of the country. Indeed many charities that focus on feeding and clothing the poor, could achieve great results, if they occasionally paid heed to the long term investments of the aforementioned kind. Raising women out of difficulties, is perhaps the only assured way of raising entire populations above the poverty line.

Mental Health

To address the mental health crisis more specifically, we can:

- Place sensory deprivation tanks across villages, poor suburbs and poverty stricken cities.

- Things that improve and protect brain health should be increased in the Muslim World, in order for the next generation to not be affected by psychological problems, that their parents had to deal with. Muslim countries must focus specifically on increasing the good foods, and decreasing the bad ones. Good ones are high in antioxidants, Omega fatty acids, low in fats and sugars; and they are don't contain hormone disruptors.

- Increasing the cultivation and consumption of cannabis plants high in CBD, and other naturally occurring chemicals that have a good impact on the mood e.g. those found in chocolate.

- Increasing taxes on sugar and sugary products, (assuming that this will reduce its consumption), and lowering taxes on meat products.

- The installation of thousands of chemical detectors across every Muslim country for immediate detection and location of illicit drugs labs, and the immediate destruction of the labs; and trial, fining and/or punishment of the perpetrators.

- The construction of anti-addiction clinics or rehabilitation centers, that are expansive, visually pleasing, filled with stimuli for physical, recreational and intellectual activities, such as swimming pools, bowling alleys, billiards tables, computer gaming facilities, library, yards for gardening and interacting with "therapy animals' etc…

Food Production and Storage

Replacing the Synthetic with the Natural

The developing world must avoid those industrial and agricultural practices that has resulted in climate change, social and sexual crisis originating in the widespread industrial use of hormone disrupting chemicals. The West's current social, political and sexual crisis can in large part be attributed to the psychopathic business practices of the previous generations. Us Muslims, and the rest of the underdeveloped world cannot afford this. If we are to choose between riches coming from Western-type industrialization, and being poor but sane - then we would have a religious obligation to choose the latter. At no point can we afford to bring about a reality in which millions of people are questioning their sexuality and already before the age of 25, they are going through hormone therapies and sex change operations. To avoid this bleak future, which has become the present reality of the West, we would have to take the following steps:

- Our food production has to be based on the principles of regenerative agriculture.

- Instead of using lab invented pesticides, we must only use chemicals that nature has known for millions of years. These are Nicotinoids, THC, Pyrethroids, Rotenoids and other botanical / plant originating / organic / home produced pesticides. The large scale use of industrial lab-invented chemicals that were not known to nature, must be outlawed, and made punishable with extreme penalties.

- To fight against swarms of insects and birds, the farmers can use the tactic of **burning** nicotine rich tobacco, high-THC cannabis and other plants high in organic pesticides and other irritant chemicals that are completely harmless to human beings, yet can prove extremely effective against such natural threats, as swarms of locusts. By burning these chemicals in- and around farmlands, complete food security for the entire population of the world can - God Willing, be made an inevitable reality. But we can do better In Shaa Allah.

- Global industrial giants have proven to be far worse of a threat to the average farmer in the developing world, then any natural threat imaginable. For local governments to thwart the evil of these giants, yet at the same time secure the benefits of modern industrial tools and practices - these governments can start renting out farming and agricultural machinery to its own farmers (e.g. for tilling the land, planting, harvesting and pest control etc.). This will prove to be a major blow to the exploitative global giants. Local engineers, universities, colleges and entrepreneurs and rich people should collaborate to design, and produce such machinery for their local/provincial needs, in order to secure the nation against the destabilizing and psychopathic global industrial and financial practices and actors. Under no circumstances, should Muslims allow for such exploitation to take root in *their* lands, and to the extent that it already has - it must be uprooted with aggressive anti-globalization policies. There is no shortage of such creative, and intelligent ideas as the one mentioned above. The developing world must capitalize on these ideas in an organized fashion, ensuring that no exploitation takes place - be it at the hands of foreign entities or local governments.

- To go a step further, we as individuals can develop a habit, that every time we go out camping, we should take some plant seeds/stones with us and plant them in places where there are nutrients, but not many plants - especial fruit bearing ones. We can also grow these plants at home, in a suitable container for a few weeks, and *then* plant them in the wild.

It should have become clear to people at this point, that no centralized governmental action against climate change is going to yield the result that we hope to see, and especially in the time frame that we wish to see it. But if we, as individuals make it a habit to plant seeds and stones, whenever we have the chance, then the 20 million trees that we would need to plant, in order to stop climate change, could be planted in less then a year time.

Hydroponics and Aeroponics

Building towers within cities for the production of food using aeroponics methods, could prove revolutionary. This could be an efficient and perhaps the only way, to prevent future disasters, which seem inevitable given the current state of local and global supply chains and infrastructure (or lack thereof).

Those unoccupied cities, buildings and houses that are abandoned, can be repurposed for aeroponics food production. Nations like China, can easily quadruple it's food production capability by turning it's ghost cities into fully automated 'food factories' - instead of allowing them to deteriorate, without having made any use of them. And even if they are not fully automated, they can easily be managed by a small number of *'post-modern farmers',* who can be educated for this purpose in less then a week time. Such simple changes, when made on a large scale, could make China the single most powerful nation in the history of humanity. This indeed, would be an example of *true* vertical farming, and appears to be one of the main practical solutions to food insecurity and extreme poverty.

The Sahara Project

The climate must be stabilized. By allowing different waters to move more freely between the different oceans, gulfs, rivers and lakes, especially on the north-south axis, we can minimize the harm done by destructive atmospheric phenomenon.

By digging rivers from the Mediterranean through North Africa, down through the Sahara Desert; then digging perpendicular to that and connecting the Red Sea to the Atlantic, then digging straight through Saudi Arabia and connecting the Persian Gulf with the Red Sea, we would be turning large dead zones into habitable, fertile grounds - both for humans and animals.

Furthermore all of the sweet water lakes and rivers can be connected on the north-south axis. The greater movement of these waters will In Shaa Allah eliminate the temperature extremes and minimize the amount and severity of destructive atmospheric phenomenon like tornadoes, hurricanes and typhoon. There is also hope that these will increase rain fall in the dry regions of the globe like the Sahara Desert.

Other important changes would be: the decline in the severity of heatwaves and sand storms, an increase in air quality and more vegetation and biodiversity across the dead zones of Earth (such as The Sahara Desert).

The greater the amount of water that can be pumped into the deserts of the globe, the more cooling can be achieved in these regions, and the average rainfall can be expected to increase by many folds. And the greater the surface area of the Earth that is covered by water, the more radiation can be reflected, and the better the weather, *and the waters* of the world can be stabilized.

A more equal distribution of water - be it sweet water or seawater, is going to be the key in closing the gap between the developing world, and the developed world. The seafood would become more accessible to people in landlocked regions that are faraway from seashores. The Sahara Project will In Shaa Allah reduce inequalities in the fishing industry and agricultural output of under-performing regions. At the same time, the rivers would serve as a great logistical solution for people living in regions that lack roads and railroads to major economic hot spots, improving the economic performance of the unprivileged.

Similar projects can be undertaken in other parts of the world:

- Australia: which, should dig rivers both on the North-south axis and East-West Axis.
- Iran can connect the Caspian sea with the Persian Gulf
- And rivers through the *Stans,* into East-Turkestan, snaking through Western China into Inner Mongolia and connecting it to the Yellow Sea.
- In the US, Connecting the Gulf of Mexico with the Pacific, by a river starting at Texas going through New Mexico, Arizona and California into the Pacific.

The actual realization of such projects, has to be made a distributed effort, if we are to succeed on time - rather then centralized in the hands of any specific government or organization: Geographers can provide guidance on the best and easiest paths that such rivers can be dug through; programmers can produce apps, which calculates the distance between the user of the app, and the nearest point of the to-be river. Average global citizens, who wish to volunteer, would install the app which shows the location, where they can travel and contribute to the effort by digging themselves and/or by providing tools, food, and fuel to those that are working there. This way the state, or provincial governments, would be spending very little money, and most of the work would be done by volunteers (who get guidance through the app designed for this purpose).

What Will This Achieve

Rivers through such scorching hot territories will lead to cooling of the regions, and thus, more rain, which would directly lead to more vegetation and biodiversity. This means, more options and opportunities for wildlife, as they (the animals) will be able to settle over a greater expanse of land, and thus, lower the probability that they would go extinct because of a lack of suitable homes. The benefits also include, the lowering of sea water levels - even if it is by a tiny percent. More vegetation will allow us more time to make the necessary changes to our lifestyle - if we are to survive till the next century. This is the only way to slow down climate change, and eventually reverse it, and to do so quickly. The more of the Earth's surface we cover with water, the more radiation the Earth will be reflecting back into space. The leveling of temperatures in regions like the Sahara Desert would also lead to more clouds which would further decrease the amount of heat being absorbed by Earth. All that is required, is that we cover a greater amount of the Earth's surface with (sea) water.

These rivers and lakes will serve as mirrors that would reflect sunlight, compensating for the decreasing reflection of the ice-covered regions such as Greenland.

The immediate benefits include a reduced risk of flooding in coastal cities, the combined populations of which reach billions. Thus, it might become the ultimate project that would bring people together, no matter their background. Instead of investing large sums of money to protect the coastal cities against rising sea level (e.g. Venice), just one percent of that sum can provide a ten fold protection, if put into the Sahara Project.

And since it is easy given that there aren't any complicated procedures involved (beyond digging) – it should be extremely cheap relative to all of the other strategies. Indeed, AI controlled vehicles can do this effortlessly. Explosives may also be applied to speed up the process. And since we will be spending money countering the chaos that is unfolding right in front of our wide open eyes, we might as well spend a tiny fraction of that to stop climate change before it is too late, and in the process make the planet more equal home for all people.

Pushing seawater inland is our only practical and plausible strategy that could work. And it is of course not sufficient that it works - rather, it must work on *time,* which humanity is running out of. The idea that we could limit our greenhouse gas emissions through global conventions is highly impractical (and perhaps even unnecessary).

On Sensitive Projects

We Muslims should not *just* be taking lessons from the technical, and scientific successes and failures of the world – but also from the organizational, cultural and linguistic achievements and failures.

Projects such as nuclear programs, missile programs, satellite programs, and other major projects, that can provide the Ummah the necessary security against the schemes of the enemies of Islam and Humanity - must be executed in accordance with the best principles of operational management. The long term well-being of the Ummah is going to require the establishment of gold and silver based economic, and financial order. Such projects then, have to be handled with utmost secrecy, and the best of risk management practices in mind. One such important lesson that Muslims have not been heeding is the practice of preventing our scholars from traveling openly, before the sensitive project is complete. Muslims have lost many bright minds to assassinations because of this recklessness. To further understand the importance of such security measures, the reader can explore the history of the Manhattan Project. For the first atomic bomb project, the US built an entire city, in which the scientists, and their families lived until the project was successfully completed.

Political and military leaders of the Muslim World can learn a great deal about operational management from projects such as the Manhattan Project, and the Apollo Program. The success of major projects depends on the level of physical protection afforded to it by the security, and armed forces of the nation. Muslim thinkers themselves, must realize that they are always a target for the enemies of Islam, and that the least they can do personally is to stop moving around daily in the open (e.g. traveling back and forth between home and work); that large number of our leaders and thinkers shouldn't congregate under one roof; that they shouldn't be communicating without the use of the best of cryptographic technology etc.

10

Conclusion

With all the difficulty I have seen in writing this book, writing the conclusion has been perhaps the most difficult. Perhaps the most productive idea I can present in these, last few paragraphs, is that, the readers should write their own conclusion based off of what has been presented in the preceding chapters. They can then share these conclusions on the internet for others to read, watch, discuss and compare.

The following are some thoughts, that I think best summarize the *implications* of the topics discussed in this book.

There are some assumption, and un-Islamic attitudes that Muslims have fallen prey to, that have been impeding our progress. Such attitudes have occasionally manifested themselves during problem solving processes, when Muslims have gathered to solve their worldly problems. Among the people that speak in these gatherings, you will find those, who usually, and quite foolishly say that they understand their religion, and that on *this* occasion, they just want to focus on the "practical issues, problems, questions, methods and strategies". This is quiet the silliness. Everyone knows intuitively that understanding is not enough. And that we must also act according to that knowledge. Despite all of our understanding, we Muslims have continued to ignore Allah, because of which Allah has allowed this suffering of the entire Ummah to continue. And no doubt, there are countless Muslims who do not understand their religion. And people who do not understand the religion of Allah, do not understand the world - and will most definitely not have the life, that they will regret not having, once they reach the end of it. All our efforts must be focused on making it easier for people to be obedient to Allah. Once that is achieved, everything else will follow In Shaa Allah.

We have to get into the practice of consulting Allah on matters of the *dunya,* by praying Istikhara, during all decision making processes. The 'u'lama should persistently remind, educate, and nurture Muslims on such noble practices of the Sahaba, and present examples of it from their lives - of how they conducted their affairs, and were taught to do Istikhara on all matters of life - whether major or minor.

Movements, causes, processes and systems don't fail because of the incompetence of the majority (of the people in it or the stakeholders), but rather because of the corruption of the minority (usually among the powerful, well educated and/or influential at an important point (place and time) in the organization. We Muslims must hold our decision makers, influencers, intellectuals, financial and industrial elite, and powerful military leaders to account for the choices that they make, and the things that they choose to pay attention to - at the cost of many other things, that they choose to ignore. In short, we must take the initiative. We must always be looking for ways to serve Allah, and His Beloved servants, no matter what the context, and our circumstances are. The ideas and strategies provided in this book, will In Shaa Allah serve as a treasure trove for Muslims, regardless of their socioeconomic circumstances, and/or their place in various organizational hierarchies that they happen to find themselves in.

CONCLUSION

From Defense To Offense

We can decide to have frontal charge against our problems and their sources. Whether the problems are behavioral, psychological, educational, economic, industrial, military or environmental – we will In Shaa Allah tackle them. The Prophet Muhammad didn't leave behind a bunch toothless, and anxious hedonists. Rather he left men and women, who upon need would sell themselves, and their families to slavery and misery, purely for the pleasure of Allah. And he, may peace and blessings be upon in the beginning and at the end, left behind men and women, the dust of whose movements - when it would become visible at a distance, was sufficient to make the empires of hedonists tremble inside their strongholds.

- The main source of evil is Iblis. If we are to succeed In Shaa Allah, we must turn *all* our guns against him, his strategies and his allies, who are his weapon by which he strikes. That is the wisest, simplest and easiest way forward.

- We must censor all the propaganda machines of the enemies of Islam, and allies of the corrupt elite. By censoring them, we are effectively destroying them, since it is profit that is enabling them to perform their devilish act of hate production. These machines include TV news channels (BBC:s, VOA:s, etc), and their social media accounts and channels.

- Hadiths, poems, ayaat and sayings of the wise should be put on the streets and buildings, and imprinted on vehicles, various different kinds of decorations, beautification items that arouse the pride, religious zeal, ambitions, competitive spirit and increase the self-esteem of Muslims - and something that will encourage them towards constructive actions. It is the job of the imams, scholars and other intellectuals to point out these ayaat, hadiths, poems, stories, proverbs and sayings and forward them to Muslim populations, organizations, design companies etc.

- We can adopt the continuous improvement mindset, by reducing complexity and undesirable variation. To do this, the various processes (regardless of the type of organization), have to be described using diagrams (e.g. cause and effects diagrams, flowcharts, mind maps…), and the important variables measured, monitored, and recorded for present, and future improvement efforts.

- Muslims must master the use of those tools, and weapons that Allah has provided us. These tools extend the reach of human beings, to the realm of the invincible. Among these tools are: the the du'a, *Allahumma Jurni fii muSeebati wa Khlufni Khairamminhu;* And *Salatul Istikhara*, on which the earlier Muslims were nurtured in consulting Allah - both during minor and major decision making processes. If they were ordered to consult Allah even on minor issues, through Istikhara, then what should the practices of those Muslims should be, who are involved in decisions made by political, military and business leaders on behalf of entire nations; And *Al Baqarah,* the second chapter of the Quran. Let us recall what the Prophet said, *"Shaitaan flees from The house in which al Baqarah is being read".* We can make it a habit, to read al Baqarah at least once a day. And always make sure, that it is read by at least one person in the house every day. It is this surah, that will serve the Muslims as an indomitable guardian of the house, of the family, and of their *emaan*, against shaitaan and his allies and tools. With this tactic shaitaan won't just be fleeing from our houses, but also from our cities and streets. It is the job of the students of knowledge to further educate, and nurture Muslims on the use of such weapons provided by Allah.

- As for those individuals who still don't know what to do, they should just focus on improving themselves. They must make themselves more competent - even if they don't have, or see absolutely any opportunity for showing, and putting to use this competence, they should still focus on making themselves intellectually, financially, spiritually, physically and rhetorically stronger, and more assertive.

Change will come, and it will come sooner rather then later In Shaa Allah as it is Allah's Promise.

> **Allah has promised, to those among you who believe and work righteous deeds, that He will, of a surety, grant them in the land, inheritance (of power), as He granted it to those before them; that He will establish in authority their religion - the one which He has chosen for them; and that He will change (their state), after the fear in which they (lived), to one of security and peace: 'They will worship Me (alone) and not associate aught with Me. 'If any do reject Faith after this, they are rebellious and wicked.** Quran 24:55

The question now is, who is going to be 'Umar of our time? And who is going to be the Khalid ibn al Waleed of our time? Who will step up, and bring this change and be remembered for the rest of time, and be rewarded for it on the Judgement Day? Who will compete for these posts, and do something real, and valuable for the Ummah, by filling the gaps in our defenses, and strengthening our offenses against people of *fasaad?*

To succeed, we Muslims must put behind the fear of failure, the fear of success, the opinions of Muslims and non-Muslims, the consequences of our love for Allah and His Messenger. We must ignore all things, and focus on the Wish of our Creator All Mighty, by puritanically following the Guidance of Muhammad, to whatever extent we can follow it, disregarding when, where, and how we fail, and how many times we fail. For us to try, *is* In Shaa Allah sufficient of an accomplishment. To try with good intentions, *is* sufficient to guarantee the Pleasure of Allah.

> **Go forth, whether light or heavy, and strive with your wealth and your lives in the cause of Allah. That is better for you, if you only knew.** Quran 9:41

And Our Last Words Are,
All Praises Belong To Allah, It is by His Permission and Grace Alone, That Good Actions Can Be Performed. May Allah's Peace and Blessings Be On His Noble Prophet Muhammad. And Indeed Peace is Only On Those, Who Have Chosen To Follow His Guidance.

Epilogue

All of the ideas, and strategies presented in this book, have to be seen in the context of all of the other ideas. While individual ideas might have their practical utility - their benefits increases exponentially, when combined with other ideas. The easiest way to improve our situation, is to jump at any opportunity for improvement that we come across. But especially the easiest ideas, which once implemented would make the distant strategies, and goals, seem more approachable.

In this volume, I have not presented all of the ideas that I had in mind. And that makes the writing of a second edition a must. Until Allah grants me success in that endeavor, I encourage all readers to focus on implementing this knowledge, and to share it with others. And to come up with their own personal strategies for strengthening the Ummah. These personal strategies can be formulated by selecting from this book those ideas that are relevant to one's own context, reordering them from the easiest ones to the most difficult ones, filling the gaps in the resulting action plan - and then setting out for action In the Name of Allah, the Merciful, the Compassionate.

Among the things not addressed in this book, are matters pertaining to security, politics, finance/banking, industry, information, and digital infrastructure. These matters will be addressed in my future works In Shaa Allah.

Go forth, whether light or heavy, and strive with your wealth and your lives in the cause of Allah. That is better for you, if you only knew. Quran 9:41

I ask Allah to put barakah in this work, and to make it the medicine that it was intended to be, and much more. All Good is from Allah, and all mistakes and sins are our own and from the shayateen.

www.ingramcontent.com/pod-product-compliance
Lightning Source LLC
Chambersburg PA
CBHW032212220526
45472CB00018B/1135